— THE —
MICROWAVE
HANDBOOK

— THE —
MICROWAVE
HANDBOOK

ENID NORMAN

CONTENTS

This edition published in 1989 by
The Hamlyn Publishing Group Limited,
a division of the Octopus Publishing Group,
Michelin House,
81 Fulham Road,
London SW3 6RB

© 1985 Hennerwood Publications Limited

ISBN 0 600 56474 6

Produced by Mandarin Offset.
Printed and bound in Hong Kong.

MICROWAVE COOKER DESIGN

Neat and compact, the microwave cooker fits conveniently on a kitchen work surface.

The microwave cooker has heralded one of the most important cooking revolutions to date. The unbelievable speed with which it can defrost frozen fare, cook fresh foods or reheat prepared dishes brings an immediacy to cooking that complies perfectly with today's time-conscious lifestyle, which is so demanding of speed and convenience.

As their benefits have become more widely recognized, so have the sales of microwave cookers increased in recent years – quite phenomenally. Yet, despite this increasing popularity, probably less is known about the design and operation of a microwave cooker than any other electronic equipment in the home. An essential difference, for instance, between microwaves and conventional cookers is that control is by time rather than temperature. Basically, a microwave is powered by electricity to produce electromagnetic (or microwave) energy at a very high frequency. These microwaves are absorbed by the food generating instantaneous heat deep inside the food cooking it rapidly and evenly. This is explained more fully in chapter 3. For the more technically minded, the illustration below describes the component parts of a standard microwave cooker and their functions.

Basic Design

■ **1. Flexible cord** with plug for an electric socket.

■ **2. Power transformer.** This increases the low domestic voltage to a very high voltage.

■ **3. High voltage rectifier and capacitor.** These further increase the high voltage and convert it to unidirectional voltage suitable for energizing the magnetron.

■ **4. Magnetron.** This device converts the electrical energy produced by the transformer-capacitor-rectifier system (described at 2 and 3 above) into microwave energy at 2450 megahertz (million cycles per second).

5. Wave guide. This is a metal channel that conducts the microwave energy from the magnetron to the cooking cavity.

6. Wave stirrer or energy distributor. This device may take several forms but in all cases its function is to reflect the microwaves emerging from the wave guide outlet and distribute them to the cooking cavity.

7. Cooking cavity. The cavity is made of metal, usually stainless steel, to prevent the escape of microwave energy and to reflect the energy assisting the heat distribution.

8. Door and frame. These are designed with special seals to guarantee that microwaves are safely confined within the cooker cavity. In addition there are built-in devices to ensure that microwave energy cuts off automatically when the door is opened. Doors usually consist of two panels of toughened glass – with a metal mesh between them. They often open from the side but on some models they drop down or slide up.

9. Vent. Usually at the top or back of the cooker, it allows moisture to escape and the magnetron cooling air to circulate.

How a Microwave Cooker Works

On/Off Control is self explanatory. When 'on' it simultaneously operates an interior light and a cooling fan. In some models there can be a few seconds' delay before the fan begins to operate. The light simply helps you see that the dish does not overcook while the cooling fan prevents the electrical components from becoming overheated and helps disperse steam and condensation.

Time Control: with microwave cooking in most cases control is by time rather than temperature. Relatively short cooking periods are required for most foods. The control is usually calibrated into 15–30 second intervals on the lower end of the scale (useful when softening butter) and in minute intervals up to 30 or 60 minutes (the longer time being needed for dishes such as stews).

Above: the time control, which is marked off in minutes.

Below: a cutaway view of a microwave cooker showing: 1. the wave guide stirrer. 2. the magnetron.

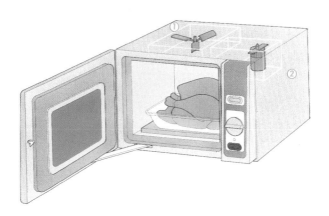

Additional Features

The range of microwave cookers at present available do incorporate many other features

Removable Floor is made of special ceramic glass and acts as a spillage tray. It is easily removed and can be washed in warm soapy water as necessary. It usually fits a few centimetres above the oven base to allow for the reflection of microwaves on to the base of the food container, as well as its other surfaces.

Defrost Control. Most microwave cookers have a defrost control. It generally works by pulsing the microwave energy on and off in a regulated pattern but in some models it simply reduces the output power. The effect of either method is an overall reduction in the microwave energy which is necessary to ensure the complete thawing of frozen foods. This control can also be used for the slow cooking of foods, such as the tougher cuts of

meat which benefit from this method.

Variable Power Control helps you to exercise more control over the speed and method of cooking. Depending on the model, it will either reduce the wattage before it enters the oven cavity, or will pulse the power on and off at varying intervals. Further information on its use and on approximate power outputs is

given on page 21.

Temperature Probe is a thermometer attached to a flexible cord with plug, which connects to a socket near the top of the cooker cavity. The probe tip is inserted into the food and the desired temperature is selected on a temperature control. The tip of the probe contains a sensor which quickly responds to heat changes within the food. The temperature is usually shown in a window on the display panel as a continuous read-out. When the required

Cook or Start Control: only when this control is set can microwaves be generated – usually there is a light on the fascia panel which indicates that cooking has started. Once set, the time indicator works back to zero and a bell, buzzer or pinger sounds, when cooking is completed.

So to use the cooker for standard operations:
1. Press the 'on' control.
2. Place the food inside and close the door.
3. Set the required time on the 'time control'.
4. Press the 'cook' or 'start' control.
5. When cooking is complete, remove the food and close the door.
6. Press the 'off' control.

Size and Power of Microwave Cookers

The size of microwave cookers varies, in both external dimensions and internal measurement of the cavity. The interior size is carefully calculated to match the output of microwave energy that the magnetron generates. This ensures the best performance and energy distribution.

in addition to those described. Some models may have one additional feature, others have several combined in their design, therefore such features are described individually.

temperature is reached the cooker switches off, or keeps the food warm on a low or 'hold' setting, thus providing the means to cook food by temperature rather than by time (as is usually the case in a microwave cooker). The temperature probe is particularly useful for roasting meat and poultry as it eliminates

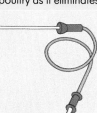

the element of estimation, which normally occurs when cooking by time alone, due to the fact that the weight, shape and starting temperature of a joint all affect the cooking time. **Turntables** are made of toughened ceramic

glass and most are easily removed for cleaning. Some microwave cookers

have a turntable instead of a stirrer, but many have both. When food is placed on the turntable the revolving action ensures that the food passes through the microwave field so that the energy is more evenly absorbed. With a few exceptions, the need to turn or rotate dishes during cooking is minimal.

Any container or food placed on a turntable must clear the walls and door of the cooker during its operation, so it is advisable to check the manufacturer's

instructions to see if they recommend that the turntable can be removed, and if the cooker can be operated effectively without it.

Rotating Antenna is usually concealed below the cooker floor, or above the ceiling and does not need to be removed. It is a circular metal disc approximately 25 cm (10 inches) in diameter, interspersed with slots. Mainly driven by air channelled from the cooling system it

distributes the microwave energy around the entire cooker cavity so that it is evenly absorbed by the food.

The following table shows how much power is used from the domestic supply to provide microwave cooking power.

Power Consumption (watts)	Approximate Output Power Supplied (watts)
1000–1100	500
1200–1300	600
1300–1400	700
1500	750

There are a few exceptions related to microwave cookers incorporating a radiant heat feature, such as a grill or convection heating, which require increased consumption.

There may also be a slight variation in the cooking power between one microwave cooker and another of the same wattage as there is with conventional cookers for which there is a recognized nominal allowance for accuracy.

Safety

Microwave cookers are rigorously tested both electrically and for microwave leakage, as described below.

The Electricity Council's BEAB label.

Electrical safety: microwave cookers are tested at the Electricity Council's Appliance Testing Laboratories to the requirements of the British Standard for household microwave cookers which is BS 3456 Part II (Section 2.33: 1976). Before this, they were tested to the draft standard and those that met the requirements were given the blue label with this wording 'Electricity Council – Approved for Safety'. This label is commonly used for catering equipment which has been tested for safety. Now, however, microwave cookers for domestic use that meet the standards will carry the familiar British Electrotechnical Approvals Board (BEAB) label.

Microwave leakage: microwave cookers intended for household use come within the scope of the Electrical Equipment (Safety) Regulations 1975 made under the Consumer Protection Act 1961. These regulations, which are enforced by local trading standards authorities, require domestic electrical equipment to be so designed and constructed that when in use it does not emit any level of radiation that could be dangerous. The sale of any appliance which allows microwave leakage at a harmful level is an offence under this Act. The safety limit for microwave leakage is set out in a British Standard (BS 5175: 1976): 'Specification for Safety of Commercial Electrical Appliances using Microwave Energy for Heating Foodstuffs'.

Tests and measurements are meticulous to ensure that safety standards are high and levels of microwave leakage low. For the mathematically minded, leakage is measured in milliwatts per square centimetre at a distance of 5 cm (2 inches) from the cooker – the maximum allowed is $5 \, mW/cm^2$. In practice, levels are usually in the order of $0.05 \, mW/cm^2$. However, even if the maximum leakage is measured, the intensity of the leakage decreases in proportion to the distance squared, so at an arm's length this would have decreased to $0.006 \, mW/cm^2$.

Some of the stringent tests conducted at the Appliance Testing Laboratories to ensure that the leakage limit is not exceeded include the following:

- The cooker door is opened and closed 100,000 times and measurements are taken after every 10,000 operations.
- The interlocks on the door are tested 100,000 times and these too are checked every 10,000 operations.
- Special attention is paid to ensure that if one interlock fails there is no way that the microwave-generator will work when the door is open.
- Mechanical strength tests are applied to the door structures and door seals to ensure they are capable of withstanding the knocks that an appliance is likely to get in normal use.
- The door seals are deliberately contaminated with oil to ensure that even if the door is not clean, microwave leakage is within the limits allowed.

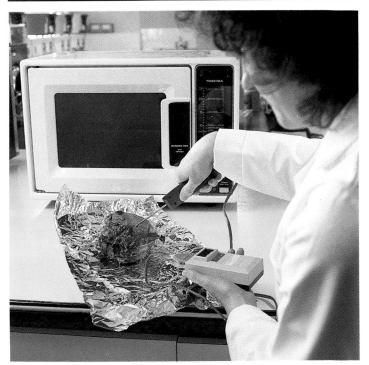

One of the tests carried out at the Appliance Testing Laboratory. The meat is being checked after standing (wrapped in foil) to verify recommended cooking times and temperatures.

There is, therefore, no possible way that microwaves can be present when the door is opened, unless the appliance is deliberately tampered with. As soon as the door catch moves a fraction the microwaves stop — just like switching a light off.

The British Standard requires manufacturers to supply instructions on maintenance for the user. These should include the manufacturer's recommended method for cleaning all seals as well as instructions for inspecting these areas for damage. They are also required to include a warning to the effect that if these areas are damaged, the appliance should not be operated until it has been repaired by a qualified service technician trained by the manufacturer.

Like many other electrical appliances, regular servicing by the manufacturer ensures that the equipment remains in good and safe working order.

How Microwaves Work

Until the introduction of microwave cookers perhaps the most familiar use of electromagnetic waves was in radio and television transmissions and radar. The principle is actually the same — electromagnetic waves are converted from electrical energy — but what is different is the size of the wavelengths produced. While broadcasting aerials transmit radio waves at a frequency of 10 megahertz per second, producing a wavelength of about 30 metres (98 feet), microwaves are generated at a frequency of about 2450 megahertz per second and, as their name 'micro' suggests, are on a much smaller scale, measuring about 12 cm (5 inches). This range of waves is illustrated on page 12.

THE ELECTROMAGNETIC SPECTRUM: Not to scale:

1 Nanometer (nm) = 10^{-9} metres

TV & Radio	1m
Microwave	0·12m
Infra Red	10^{-4}m
Ultra Violet	10nm
X Ray	10^{-2}nm
Higher Radiations	10^{-4}nm

The range of electro-magnetic waves, showing where the microwaves fit in.

Using Microwaves

Non-ionising energy: As with broadcasting and radar waves, microwave energy is invisible and a non-ionising form of electro-magnetic energy. These non-ionising waves of energy do not produce biological changes upon exposure except in very high densities.
Ionising rays: Microwaves are non-accumulative and should not be confused with ionising rays, such as X-rays, gamma-rays or ultra-violet, which are known to cause irreversible chemical and cellular changes with little or no temperature change.

Safety and Economy

Microwaves have several remarkable qualities that make them safe and economical for cooking – they can be reflected, transmitted and absorbed.

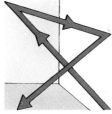

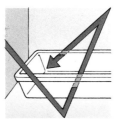

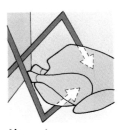

Reflection:
Microwaves cannot pass through metal, they are reflected by it. For this reason cookers are designed with metal cavities, so that microwaves can bounce off the metal surfaces and yet be confined within the cavity. The three diagrams demonstrate this with one wave, although there are, of course, several thousand.

Transmission:
Microwaves can pass through certain materials, such as glass, china, paper, some natural fibres and some plastics without actually heating them, as they are devoid of substances which absorb microwave energy (although some are heated by conducted heat from the food itself).

Absorption:
Microwaves can be absorbed by moisture molecules – water, fat and sugar within the food. These molecules vibrate at the same speed as the frequency, which is over two thousand million times per second, and produce intense frictional heat so rapidly that they speed up any cooking process.

Different Food Types

The instant penetration of microwave energy is from all surfaces of the food and as this occurs heat is generated, and as continuing energy is applied, it will pass to the next layer and so on throughout the food.

The initial penetration of microwaves is approximately 2.5–4 cm (1–1½ inches). However there is not an identical depth of penetration for all foods, but there is an equivalent depth of microwave penetration depending on the composition of each food type, e.g. whether it is porous or dense.

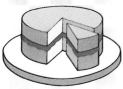 

Porous foods: Foods, such as sponge cakes and puddings, are 'porous' and will absorb microwave energy rapidly, as the tiny air pockets within the structure of such foods offer no resistance to rapid penetration.

Dense foods: Food with a closely-packed molecular structure represents a dense food which will absorb the microwave energy at a slower rate. Take, for example, a joint of meat: if you were to slice through it, you would see how closely interwoven the meat fibres were. This density reduces the initial depth of microwave penetration, together with the outer surface heat, so consequently the time it takes for heat to pass throughout the food is lengthened accordingly.

By comparison an oven-ready chicken of the same weight will cook faster than the joint of meat. The air space in the centre of the bird does not absorb any energy but simply allows it to pass through. So, despite the weights being the same, the cooking time varies, because the density and structure of the food is different.

ADVANTAGES OF THE MICROWAVE COOKER

Microwave cookers are now used by a very broad section of the community. Men and women of all ages and with widely differing eating preferences and habits are discovering the many advantages – including versatility, economy and speed – which microwave cooking offers.

Versatility

Independent of other cooking equipment, microwave cookers can thaw, heat, boil, bake, roast, steam or poach foods. They can also simplify recipe preparation work by softening fats, dissolving jelly cubes, melting chocolate, and reheating small amounts of liquid very speedily.

The other main aspect of their versatility is their use in the reheating of food, for which they give excellent results. For families who have an irregular meal routine, this is a great advantage as plate meals can be quickly and efficiently reheated. Unlike traditional methods of reheating, the moisture is retained within the food which does not dry out or change colour. It is also considerably less expensive to reheat by microwave than it is to preheat a conventional cooker in order to warm up food – food can be reheated in seconds or a few minutes depending on the quantity involved.

Fuel Economy

Microwave cookers broadly speaking will cook food at between one-quarter and one-third of the time taken by conventional cookers, see the chart on page 16. (There are variations depending on the starting temperature, density and quantity of food being cooked.) And because the microwave method of defrosting, heating and cooking is controlled by a timer, not by temperature, the majority of the electrical power is used only during the timed period, no preheating is needed, and this, together with the low consumption, is a very positive form of fuel economy.

When cooking is completed, the microwave switches off, although the food continues to cook by its absorbed heat.

It is important that times recommended by the manufacturer are followed as they are related to the output power of the oven.

Food Economy

The microwave cooker is especially useful for family meals. It reheats the food quickly keeping it moist and appetizing.

Some foods, such as vegetables and fruit, can be cooked with less water than on a conventional hob and therefore retain more of their nutrients, colour and flavour.

Food can be taken straight from the freezer to be defrosted and cooked in the microwave.

Moreover, small portions of left-over cooked foods, such as rice, pasta, fruit, soups or sauces can be frozen and then easily defrosted and used for any combination of recipes at any time. Similarly, surplus vegetables, or individual portions of pudding can be refrigerated and reheated the following day and with only minimal loss of flavour.

Time Economy

Many foods can be cooked in the microwave in the container from which they are to be served (provided they are microwave-safe, see page 28). Also, prepared foods can be heated on, or in, the serving plate or dish, which considerably reduces the amount of washing up. With a well-stocked freezer and a microwave cooker, a wide variety of meals can be prepared with very little forward planning.

Cool Work

Heat is produced in the food, which is confined within the cooker cavity and so the surrounding areas do not get hot. This, in turn, helps minimize any smells from the food during the brief cooking period.
Also, the kitchen remains cool and pleasant to work in and, without atmospheric heat and fumes, it stays cleaner for a much longer period.

Mobility

Most microwave cookers are compact and mobile and can be positioned at a convenient level on a table or work surface. They usually only require a 13 amp plug and socket outlet so, unlike conventional cookers, they can be moved to rooms other than the kitchen. Holiday homes, patios, dining rooms and granny flats are all areas where the microwave cooker can be used, providing the

A comparison of cooking times and amount of power used in a microwave cooker and a conventional electric cooker

Food	Cooker	Input Power (watts)	Pre-heat	Cooking Time	Approx. Power Consumption
1.5 kg (3–3½ lb) roast chicken	Electric oven	2500	20 mins 200°C, 400°F	80 mins	2½ units
	Microwave	1400	Nil	21–25 mins	½ unit
2 jacket potatoes	Electric oven	2500	20 mins 200°C, 400°F	50–60 mins	2 units
	Microwave	1400	Nil	10–11 mins	¼ unit
Lemon sponge pudding	Electric hob	1000	8 mins (to boil)	90 mins (to simmer)	¼ unit
	Microwave	1400	Nil	5 mins	⅛ unit

The comparison of energy consumption and cooking times can only be approximate due to the many variations between both conventional and microwave cookers.
These statistics are based on a 700 watt output power microwave cooker, working at a constant full power, and an average domestic electric cooker.

correct electrical supply is available. All a microwave needs is a good air space round it and to be positioned away from any direct source of heat so that the cooling system can operate efficiently. The air temperature should be approximately 40°C/104°F.

The only exceptions to portable models are those designed specifically for 'built-in' kitchens, or those which are an integral part of a conventional gas or electric cooker.

Placed on a trolley, the microwave cooker is easily transportable and can be plugged in wherever it is most convenient.

Easy Maintenance

Cleaning is greatly reduced as only a warm soapy cloth is needed to remove any particles of food which spatter on to the cooker walls or base. It is important to wipe any spillage, for this would otherwise continue to absorb energy and heat up as a result, becoming carbonized and difficult to remove, see page 87.

Help for the Disabled

In some cases it is possible for registered blind people to have a specially marked fascia panel fitted to their microwave. This must first be discussed with the manufacturer as he has to supply the Royal Institute for the Blind with a blank panel so that the Institute can mark it accordingly.

Actually, microwaves have proved a boon to many disabled people. There is little chance of being burned as the oven itself does not get hot and — because microwave cookers are usually positioned at work level height — opening and closing of the door is much easier than with a conventional cooker.

MICROWAVE FACTS

Microwave cookery has as we have already discovered, a great advantage of speed over conventional cooking but in order to make the most efficient use of your time, it is worth spending a little while studying the new cooking methods and different techniques, which a microwave cooker demands. These techniques are not complicated and many have keen similarities to conventional methods. Let us compare the two methods.

Conventional Oven

In a conventional oven the air is heated to a pre-selected temperature either by the electric elements or by the burning of gas. With both types of heating the hot dry air which surrounds the food begins by cooking the outer surfaces and the heat is gradually conducted towards the centre. Because of the time this process takes, the outer surface usually becomes dry and crisp.

Conventional Hob

When using the hob for frying, the heat from the element or flame is transferred to the pan and in turn to the food.

Cooking starts at the point where the heat touches the pan and because of the high temperature of the fat and the direct contact, fried foods become crisp on the under surface. They need to be turned over to ensure even cooking. For the same reason, foods cooked in a saucepan need to be stirred.

A table to show which foods are not suitable for microwave cooking.

Not suitable	Reason for limitation
Foods fried in deep fat	*You cannot control the temperature of fat for frying.*
Food with a batter coating	*Batter will not become crisp.*
Yorkshire puddings, pancakes	*They require a hot surface on which to set.*
Some rich fruit cakes	*Size of oven restricts container size, which should only be half full of mixture. A fruit cake requires low variable setting for good results.*
Eggs cooked in their shells	*The shell is porous. Microwaves penetrate instantly and heat the air chamber. The rapid expansion of gas quickly bursts the shell.*
Large quantities e.g. 12 jacket potatoes	*The size of the cooker cavity restricts the amount of food that can be cooked at any one time. Unless the potatoes are all of even weight and size, they will cook unevenly. They have to be done 4 at a time, which eliminates the time gain.*
Very large turkey	*Most ovens will not take a large bird. Food should never touch any of the walls and allowance has to be made for turning birds several times during the cooking period. The ideal load for most cookers is under 6 kg (12 lb).*

Microwave Cookers

The different appearance of cooked food
Food absorbs microwave energy from all directions and instantaneous penetration occurs below all exposed surfaces. The food then is cooked by frictional heat, not by contact with hot air or a hot pan. This rapid form of heating leaves the surface of the food moist, not dry and crisp, which accounts for the difference in appearance from foods cooked conventionally. For example, poultry will be moist and tender but will not have a crisp brown skin; cakes will be light in texture, but will not have a golden brown crust. There are simple techniques to overcome such differences, as will be explained in detail on page 26.

The limitations of a microwave cooker Some foods and some methods of cooking are simply not suitable for a microwave cooker. These items and the reasons why they are unsuitable are listed in the table on page 18. They are best cooked conventionally.

Cooking time The greatest difference between the two methods of cooking is that all cooking has to be measured by time in a microwave oven, although a microwave thermometer can also be used in conjunction with the time control. If variable power or defrost power is used, it is also measured in time. These two controls do actually reduce the amount of microwave energy absorbed (see page 12) but as far as the cook is concerned, they are regulated in minutes.

It is important to know the output power of your cooker, so that you know whether to adjust the timings given in recipes (other than those that come from the manufacturer of

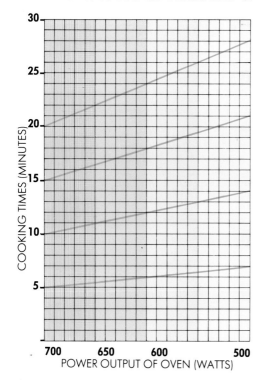

A chart to show the difference in timing related to output

As most meats and poultry require a longer standing period than most other foods, these are best covered in foil **after** removal from the oven to keep in all the heat, so that they can be served without reheating. Keep the meat in its cooking dish and wrap the foil around the sides of the dish to form a tight tent shape. This lengthened standing time with roasts makes carving easier as the muscle fibres relax during this period. If a dish has been covered with a lid or cling film during its cooking, it should stay covered during its standing time.

your cooker). The output is given in the instruction manual; if not, it is usually indicated on the side or back of the cooker.

You will probably prefer to keep referring to the instruction manual during the first few months of use, or at least until you have gained some experience. As the timings are memorised and confidence grows, you will undoubtedly wish to try other recipes from the growing variety of microwave cookery books now available.

Most books on general sale give reference to the output power of the cooker in which the recipes have been developed and tested. These may well differ from your own cooker, and for this reason the chart below under the heading of variable power, should help with any timing adjustments which may be necessary. There are fractional differences between, say, a 600 and 700 watt on timings, but there is a noticeable difference between a 500 watt and 700 watt, particularly on protracted timings. The lower the output power, the longer the cooking time necessary. So if, for example, a recipe states that you should cook a dish for 5 minutes in a cooker with a 700 watt output, you will see from the table that the dish will need $5\frac{1}{2}$ minutes with a 650 watt output, 6 minutes with a 600 watt and 7 minutes with a 500 watt. Correct timings are important, if not critical, if first class results are to be achieved.

Standing time Even after the microwave energy has been switched off and the food removed from the cooker, there is often an additional amount of cooking time to be taken into account. It is known as standing time. During this period the heat created by microwave friction continues to conduct itself throughout the food and so equalizes the temperature. Cooking does not stop immediately the microwave cooker does; it can be likened to a bouncing ball which takes a while to stop after the last time it has been hit.

It is for this reason that some foods are removed while appearing slightly under-cooked, to allow the completion of cooking during the standing time. If for any reason after this period the food still requires additional microwave time, it is very simple to heat again, but there is no remedy for overcooked food. The length of standing time varies with recipes and is chiefly dependent on the weight, density and composition of the food. You do not need to repeat the standing time if any extra cooking is needed.

Using the Power

The measured output power of the cooker is the amount of available energy within the oven cavity for such operations as cooking, heating or defrosting.

Full/High/Maximum power This is continuous, uninterrupted power and is used for the majority of recipes. Where variable power is not available it is also used for reheating.

Defrost power A freezer provides the perfect complement to a microwave cooker. In combination they provide many advantages, the most convenient of which is that the microwave eliminates the need to leave foods out to defrost hours before they are cooked, which also overcomes the problem of forgetting to take them out of the freezer at all.

The next most important advantage is that defrosting food by this method is so quick that it considerably reduces loss or deterioration of flavour.

When the defrost control is in operation, the microwave energy is pulsed 'on' and 'off' in a regulated pattern. On the lower output models it usually works at 50% of full power and on higher output models at 30–40%.

The reason this control is necessary is to ensure that foods are defrosted slowly and without the cooking process being started. Ice crystals do not form evenly throughout food, despite the quick freezing process. Converting this uneven formation of the ice to moisture has to be done slowly. The 'ON AND OFF' programme automatically produced by the defrost control, gives just the right amount of heat to make even thawing of food possible. Without this degree of control, the food would tend to start cooking on the surfaces before the slow conduction of heat reached the centre, which would remain icy.

In many models the 'DEFROST' control is incorporated as part of the variable power control. In others it is a separate control and some do not have such a control at all. For models without a 'DEFROST' control (generally the earlier makes) the same principle can be applied by turning the cooker on and off manually to give brief interspersed periods of microwave energy. It is advisable to work on a one minute cycle of energy with a two minute standing time for small products and three minutes of energy plus five minutes' standing time for dense foods.

Variable power control This control adjusts the amount of microwave energy released into the oven cavity over a timed period and so allows for variation in the speed of cooking. The energy is automatically cycled 'ON' and 'OFF' for varying lengths of time depending on power setting. This gives more flexibility to cooking, allowing foods to be cooked by the most suitable method.

The lower power settings use little energy, but as you move to higher settings, the amount of energy increases.

The similarity between the conventional oven and the microwave cooker is that the lower the temperature or setting, the longer the food takes to cook; the higher the setting, the shorter the cooking time. Also you can reduce or increase the power by adjusting the control at any time during the sequence.

To date there is no standard manufacturer's definition for what variable power is, so it is described and determined in different ways. Some manufacturers show these power levels in numerical form from 1–10; others by defining the amount of energy such as LOW, DEFROST, MEDIUM, MEDIUM HIGH, HIGH AND FULL; and the remainder in cooking terms as WARM, DEFROST, SIMMER, STEW, BAKE, ROAST, REHEAT and HIGH.

The chart below shows the approximate power outputs for the different variable power settings for 700–650–600 watt cookers, together with a description of settings given in various popular microwave cookers.

Variable output control microwave cookers are becoming increasingly popular and some incorporate electronic touch control where any percentage power level can be selected.

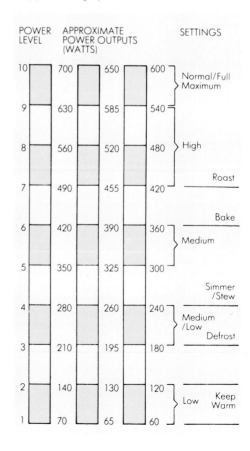

POWER LEVEL	APPROXIMATE POWER OUTPUTS (WATTS)			SETTINGS
10	700	650	600	Normal/Full Maximum
9	630	585	540	
8	560	520	480	High
7	490	455	420	Roast
6	420	390	360	Bake
5	350	325	300	Medium
4	280	260	240	Simmer /Stew
3	210	195	180	Medium /Low Defrost
2	140	130	120	Low Keep Warm
1	70	65	60	

Factors Which Affect Microwave Cooking

There are various factors concerning the food itself, as described below, which have to be taken into account before starting to cook by microwave.

Shape Foods which are uniform in shape are ideal as they absorb energy at an even rate. In both conventional and microwave cookers, thin areas of food will cook faster than thicker parts, but this can be controlled to a degree in microwave cooking. The perimeter of the container is where the food

receives the most initial energy, so by placing the thick areas of food to the outside of the container and the thinner parts to the centre, where they receive slightly less energy, the cooking or heating process is more evenly balanced.

The same principles of arrangement should also be followed when reheating plated meals as shown in the photograph.

Temperature The temperature of the food before it is cooked influences the cooking or heating time necessary. Low temperature foods require a longer period of cooking than any at room temperature, so allow for this if you use foods straight from the refrigerator.

With the exception of vegetables, all frozen food should be defrosted before cooking, unless manufacturers' instructions specify otherwise.

Size Smaller portions of food will cook more quickly than larger portions, both in conventional and microwave cookers. If you are cooking several of the same items at a time, they should be reasonably equal in size, weight and shape, so that they will cook at an even rate. If they are very irregular in form, the cooking will be uneven.

Quantity As you increase the volume of food being cooked, so you must increase the time. This is necessary because the amount of energy remains constant, but has to be shared among an increased volume of food

Plated meals should be so arranged that thick foods, such as chicken portions and potatoes, are around the outside of the plate and vegetables, such as sweetcorn, beans, or peas towards the centre where they receive less energy. Such meals should be covered with cling film with one edge loosened prior to heating.

Cling film should be lightly pierced with a sharp knife or be loosened at one corner to allow steam to escape and prevent 'ballooning' as the gas is expanding.

A loose cover, such as a paper towel, non-stick silicone paper or greaseproof paper, keeps meat, poultry and bacon from spattering over the oven walls.

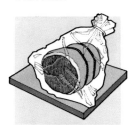

As an alternative roasting bags can be used with the open ends loosely secured by string or a rubber band. They can also be split down one side and used to cover the meat loosely. Plastic cook-in bags are good for vegetables.

and therefore requires a longer period of time to take effect.

The increase depends to some extent on the composition of the food. For instance, if you doubled the volume of dense foods, you would almost have to double the time, but for light-textured foods you would increase by just half as much time again. It is best to check the results before the end of the cooking period, so that you under rather than over-cook the food and can then extend the cooking time as necessary.

Composition Foods which have a high content of fat or sugar heat at a faster rate and reach a higher temperature than water-based foods.

High-moisture foods, such as meat and vegetables, take longer to cook than those with little water, such as cakes and bread.

Bone conducts heat in food, so any areas of meat next to the bone will cook very quickly and often cause an uneven cooking result. The most successful results are those where the bone has been removed, the meat rolled and tied into a compact shape with string.

Microwave Cooking Techniques

Covering foods As in conventional cooking, covering foods with a cover or lid traps in the steam and moisture, so helping to tenderize the food and speed the cooking. It is recommended for cooking vegetables, stews, casseroles and when reheating foods other than bakery items. Many microwave containers have integral lids but, if not, a suitable inverted plate or cling film can be used.

Stirring food This technique is used for both conventional and microwave cookery, to distribute heat evenly. Stirring avoids over-cooking the outer edges of the food and helps to distribute the heat more quickly to the centre. The number of times it is necessary to stir depends on the volume of food being cooked and this is usually mentioned specifically where appropriate in a recipe.

Turning food Applied to microwave cooking, this can either mean turning over or turning around.

It is necessary to turn over dense foods, such as meat and poultry, to equalize the heat during cooking. Exceptions to this rule would be if they are being cooked by means of a temperature probe or in a model incorporating a turntable.

Turning around is moving the position of the container during cooking and is recommended by some manufacturers for the cooking of cakes, again to equalize the amount of cooking in different parts.

There is no general rule about when to turn food because of the differences between models of microwave ovens, but there is less likelihood of this being necessary in models with a turntable or rotating antenna. After a

Unevenly shaped food, for instance chicken drumsticks, small whole fish, chops, should be arranged in the dish with the thinner parts to the centre, where they receive less energy.

Small items of the same food, such as fairy cakes, should be arranged in a ring towards the outside of a round dish.

little practice, however, you will easily be able to judge for yourself if the food is cooking evenly and, if it is not, you can just turn the container slightly to overcome the problem.

Arranging food When several individual items of the same food, for example baked eggs, are to be cooked, arrange them in a ring pattern with a space between each, leaving the centre of the ring empty.

Releasing pressure in food Any foods which have a tight fitting skin or membrane must be pricked with a fork or toothpick prior to cooking. If you do not do this the skin will burst as steam builds up within during cooking. This can be applied to jacket potatoes, sausages, chicken livers, egg yolks, tomatoes, some fruits, and apples, which are scored.

Shielding food Sensitive areas of food need protection from full microwave energy in order to prevent overcooking. Small strips of aluminium foil can be wrapped around such vulnerable areas as the wing tips, drumsticks and tail end of poultry, sometimes small areas of breast, the heads and tails of whole fish, and the thinner end of a leg of lamb (see page 28).

As aluminium foil reflects microwave energy, these protected areas, which need to be cooked at a slower rate, do not get cooked by microwave energy but by heat conducted from other parts of the food. You can either add the foil at the start of the cooking process and remove it halfway through, or you can add it when required to any parts of food which appear to be cooking at a faster rate than the rest.

The amount of foil used should be small compared to the total surface area of the food and should not touch the walls of the oven, for this could cause 'arcing' (see page 93) across the cavity.

Use a fork to prick the skins of jacket potatoes before cooking.

25

A selection of the various ways of enhancing the appearance of cakes cooked in the microwave.

Removing cooking juices Juices of certain foods, particularly roast meat and poultry, are released during cooking, and as they continue to attract microwave energy they can eventually dry out. It is advisable to remove such juices at regular intervals during cooking and use them for making gravy.

Browning food Since there is little applied surface heat in a microwave cooker, food does not readily colour to any degree, particularly during the short cooking times. Some foods, however, will brown lightly over an extended time period, and this is more likely to occur with large pieces of meat with a good covering of fat; in poultry which has pockets of fat under the skin; with minced meat and its suspended distribution of fat, and bacon with its combination of fat and brine. A slight chemical change takes place on the surface, but because of the speed at which they cook the depth of colour is lighter than that achieved by conventional means. To achieve the traditional colour just transfer the roast to your conventional oven for ten minutes.

Small items of food such as chops, cutlets, steaks, sausages and chicken portions which need less cooking time will not brown and so will not have an attractive appearance. Fortunately such limitations can be overcome.

■ For small meat and poultry items a browning dish will sear the surfaces of the meat and so provide an attractive grilled effect (see page 33 for details on how to use a browning dish or skillet).

■ A variety of coating mixes and seasoned browning sauces is now available, made specifically for microwave cookery.

■ Many browning or coating agents can be mixed at home. Try using a mixture of butter and paprika for poultry.

■ For meat joints try brushing a mixture of soy sauce and brown sugar or equal quantities of tomato ketchup and brown sauce over all surfaces before cooking. There is a degree of salt in these foods but not sufficient to alter the texture of the meat.

▓ Redcurrant jelly, cranberry sauce or honey will add both flavour and a mild colour to suitable foods.

▓ Try coating chicken portions with crushed crisps or savoury biscuits before they are cooked.

▓ Add a few drops of browning to enrich the appearance of meat casseroles.

A variety of different toppings and glazes for bread cooked in the microwave.

The limitations of browning also affect foods such as cakes, biscuits and bread, although not to quite the same extent. By using a coloured mixture for cakes and biscuits, for instance chocolate, coffee, ginger or mixed spices, many of the problems are overcome. If, however, a recipe calls for a plain cake or biscuit mixture, the following methods will help to disguise its pale appearance.

▓ A colourful frosting or icing can be used.

▓ The cake can be lightly brushed with warm jam and rolled in desiccated or toasted coconut.

▓ Icing sugar, chopped nuts or a mixture of cinnamon and sugar can be sprinkled on top.

▓ To add additional colour to small individual cakes, chopped glacé cherries, finely chopped crystallized fruit, chopped walnuts, sultanas or chocolate polka dots or chips can be added to the mixture before cooking.

To give additional colour to the pale appearance of bread made in the microwave cooker the following hints may prove useful.

▓ Before cooking, brush the bread with a little diluted beef extract and sprinkle with either poppy seeds, toasted sesame seeds, nibbed wheat or finely chopped nuts.

▓ For any bread made with wholemeal flour, brush with a little milk and sprinkle with buckwheat, rolled oats or porridge oats.

▓ Individual rolls can be brushed with beaten egg to give an additional glaze.

▓ For savoury breads, brush the surface with a little beaten egg and sprinkle with grated cheese, dried herbs, caraway seeds or chopped nuts.

▓ Alternatively bread, once it has been cooked, can be browned under a preheated conventional grill.

COOKING DISHES & UTENSILS

Always check first with your manufacturer's handbook, but most will agree that **small** pieces of foil can be used to shield particular areas of food in the microwave.

When choosing cooking dishes and utensils for the microwave cooker, the most important consideration is what the container is made of and the next is its shape. The containers should be made of materials which allow microwaves to pass straight through to the food. They should not contain properties which may reflect or absorb them.

Suitable materials can be found in most household cupboards often among those in everyday use. These include dishes, bowls or cups made of glass, china, glazed earthenware or stoneware, so it is worthwhile just checking what you have on the shelves before you purchase any new containers made specifically for microwave cooking.

In addition such natural fibres as cotton, linen, wood, straw baskets and paper can be used for brief heating periods. These are considered individually on the following pages, but these simple guidelines will help in the choosing of the correct container.

■   Ensure that containers do not have any metallic trim, either in the form of decoration or in the printing underneath or in the screwed-on handles. Avoid glued-on handles, too, as some adhesives will heat and eventually melt.

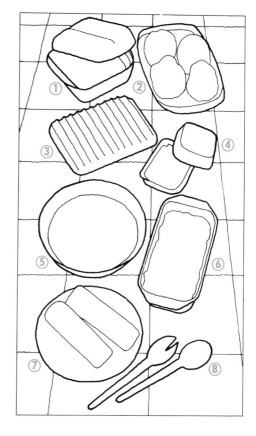

A selection of special microwave ware.
1. Vegetable dish with divided lid. 2. Baking dish. 3. Roasting rack. 4. Side dish with cover. 5. Flan dish. 6. Loaf container. 7. Shallow dish. 8. Cooking utensils.

Above: Glass jugs for sauces and glass dishes for gentle baking are suitable for use in the microwave. *Middle*: China (without any metal content) comes in a variety of shapes and can be used in the microwave.

■ Whenever possible use a round or ring-shaped container with a straight rather than curved side to ensure uniform heating.

■ Ring moulds are ideal for savoury meat rings, terrines, mousses or cakes. These can easily be improvised by standing a plain glass tumbler in the centre of a round dish. Hold it in position while you add the mixture.

■ In square and rectangular shaped containers, the food is unevenly spread, particularly in the corners. These areas tend to heat first and therefore become overcooked by the time the food in the middle is ready. This can be partly overcome by folding small pieces of foil round the corner edges, so that the microwave energy will be deflected away from the vulnerable spots (see page 28). The foil can be removed halfway during the cooking if necessary.

■ Oval dishes will have a similar problem but to a far lesser degree. They are suitable shapes for defrosting and cooking whole fish and reheating casserole foods.

■ Always choose a deeper container when cooking foods which need a 'rolling boil' action, such as pasta and rice.

■ Never heat liquids in narrow-necked containers. As the microwaves produce heat below the surface, natural gases tend to build up, so adequate space must be allowed for these to escape freely.

■ When defrosting or heating frozen foods with a high liquid content, such as sauces and soups, place the frozen food into a compact container, so that as the liquid melts on the outside it is close to the frozen portion. If a container is too wide the liquid runs in a thin stream over the base of the dish and will continue to heat before the remainder of the food has absorbed sufficient energy.

■ Cover foods which contain a lot of liquid, such as soups, stews, casseroles, curries, vegetables, steamed puddings, peeled fruit and frozen foods, during cooking.

■ Do *not* cover foods which are preferred firm and 'dry' such as pastry, cakes, bread, vegetables or fruit in their skins, such as a jacket potato or a baked apple.

■ To make your own substitute for a special meat roasting rack, invert a small china plate in the centre of a suitably sized baking dish. This will raise the meat above its own juices.

If ever in doubt about the suitability of a container just follow this simple test:
Place 250 ml (8 fl oz) of water in a glass jug and put this in the centre of the dish.
Heat on Maximum (Full) power for one minute. The water should be hot and the container cool. If the container becomes hot it should *NOT* be used.

Above: Stoneware with an all-over glaze can be used in the microwave. Check that it is suitable before purchasing.

Glass

Ovenware glass is particularly suitable for microwave cooking and can be used indefinitely. Jugs can be used for cooking sauces and heating liquids; basins for puddings; flan cases for pastry; larger mixing bowls for cooking of rice, pasta and preserves and small casseroles for vegetables and fruit.
Plain glass can be used for gentle heating, but not for foods which contain a high proportion of sugar and fats, for at very high temperatures they could crack from the conducted heat of the contents.
Avoid the use of lead crystal altogether.

China

China is another good material for use in microwave cooking. Cups and mugs can be used for drinks; casserole dishes for fish, meat and poultry recipes; plates for reheating meals; soufflé dishes for cake making; individual ramekins for starters and chilled desserts; individual bowls for porridges, soups and baked apples; shallow casseroles for fruit crumbles and vegetable bakes.
Before using just check that the china has no metal content (see page 28).

Earthenware and Stoneware

Earthenware and stoneware utensils can be used just as successfully as china providing they have an *all over glaze*. If they are unglazed, they are porous and if used, would share the microwave energy with the food instead of allowing it to pass through. Effectively this both makes the container very hot and slows down the cooking operation.
Check that they are suitable before purchase.

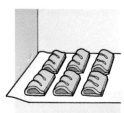

When reheating pastry items, sit them on plain white kitchen paper towelling to absorb excess moisture from the pastry.

Hamburgers or other hand-held snacks can be heated on, then served in, a plain white serviette.

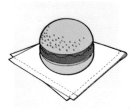

Chocolate boxes, provided they are not wax coated, make interesting containers when baking cakes.

Paper

Kitchen paper towelling has many uses both under and over food as it absorbs excess fat or moisture. Use plain white paper towels to avoid colour transfer to the food. Place a sheet on the base of the cavity when reheating individual pastry items, such as sausage rolls, or to cook a jacket potato. Such methods will reduce sogginess at the base of the food. Use it in a double thickness to dry herbs for storage, or flower petals to make a potpourri. It can also be used as a loose cover to prevent foods from spattering on to the oven walls.

Plain white serviettes are useful for heating snacks which are going to be held in the hand to eat, such as a salt beef sandwich, hot dogs or hamburgers.

Plates, cups and shallow cooking dishes manufactured in a tough paper are available and can be used for short heating periods. This paper is generally porous and foods containing high fat or sugar content should not be used in them.

Paper baking cases are suitable for individual cakes but should be used two at a time to support the food mixture during the cooking due to the rapid heat expansion. The outer case can be reused at a later date.

Chocolate and confectionery cardboard boxes, if lined with cling film, can be used for cooking light-textured cakes. These provide the opportunity for some unusual shapes. Wax-coated containers are not suitable for microwave cooking as the high temperature reached would cause the wax to melt.

Ovenable paperboard is now being used as a commercial container by some food manufacturers and directions for use are given both for microwave and conventional cookers. A limited amount of this material is available through retail outlets, in such forms as shallow trays, individual cake dishes, and plates, all of which are suitable for microwave cookers. Read the instructions before using.

Greaseproof or non-stick silicone paper can also be used to cover foods which might spatter. It can be cut to size to line the base of cake dishes, or used as a sheet on which to cook biscuits and cookies.

Cotton and Linen Napkins

Cotton and linen napkins can be used for briefly warming bread rolls. If you slightly dampen the napkins and warm for a few seconds, they can be served with foods which are eaten with the fingers, such as spare ribs or prawns in their shells.

However, make absolutely certain that they are pure fibres and have no synthetic properties. Unless you are sure of this, they should not be used.

Wood and Straw Baskets

Wooden utensils, such as spoons, can be used for stirring sauces; wooden bowls can be used for brief reheating of foods. Straw baskets are useful for reheating bread rolls. If such materials are used for longer times they would be likely to crack or char. Make sure that neither metal staples nor glue have been used in their construction.

Natural shells

Sea shells will transmit microwave energy to the food. Scallop shells are particularly attractive used for fish starters.

Plastics

Some plastic materials are very useful in microwave cooking and play an essential part in easy preparation.
Roasting bags: can be used for the cooking of meat joints and poultry and the blanching of potatoes before roasting in a conventional oven. Metal ties should not be used, the ends can be loosely secured with an elastic band or string.
Polythene bags: can be used for the cooking of vegetables or blanching for subsequent storage in the freezer.
Cook-in bags: frozen convenience foods are often prepacked in these. Providing they are slit on the top to prevent bursting during cooking they can be safely used in the microwave cooker.
Cling film: can be used to cover foods or to line some containers. Pierce the cling film if used as a cover to prevent ballooning during the heat expansion.
Foam cups: are suitable for use when short cooking or heating times are used.
Melamine: is not recommended for use as it absorbs microwave energy, which results in distortion and cracking of the material which is irreversible.

Special Microwave Cookware

These utensils can be either glass ceramic or hard thermoplastic materials plainly indicated for microwave use and dishwasher safe! Such materials will withstand reasonably high temperatures as they have been designed for specific use in the microwave cooker; they therefore come in a range of suitable shapes and sizes, with a variety of special uses.
Microwave browning dish This ceramic dish is specially designed for microwave cooking. It has a coating on the bottom which absorbs the microwave energy, and causes the surface to reach grilling temperature while the

sides remain relatively cool. Food placed on the hot surface will sear as if in a hot frying pan. It is then cooked both by microwave energy and the heat from the dish. Foods are turned over during cooking as in conventional methods. There are two distinct designs, a flat grill tray and a skillet, which is a shallow casserole dish with a lid. The former has a well round the rim of the dish which catches the fat and juices, as the meat cooks, so that it does not steam in its own juices. This method is good for browning small pieces of meat, such as steaks, chops, cutlets and hamburgers. It can also be used for frying eggs, grilling sandwiches and many other foods which require a hot surface for cooking. The skillet can be used for browning onions, diced vegetables and chicken portions. It's also useful for making sauces or gravies from the cooking liquids after the meat has browned. The manufacturers of the browning dish give a comprehensive guide for the preheating times and subsequent cooking times necessary for its use, and this is included with each purchase.

One thing has to be remembered, however, as the browning dish becomes very hot, it is necessary to use oven gloves when handling.

Microwave roasting rack This rack of either ceramic or hard plastic is designed to raise meats and poultry above their own juices as they are cooking. It is also used for heating breads and rolls. A similar design with an integral drip tray is available for bacon.

Microwave popper/steamer/roaster This is a versatile container which can be used for popping corn, steaming vegetables and puddings or roasting small joints.

Microwave baking moulds A ring-shaped dish between 7.5 and 10 cm (3 and 4 inches) deep with a hollow centre or a centre coil. This shape allows maximum exposure to microwave energy and is ideal for cakes, savoury meats and moulds.

Microwave muffin pans Approximately 20 cm (10 inches) in diameter, these have five or six divided moulds which are suitable for cooking small cakes, baked eggs and individual starters.

Microwave thermometers Regular meat thermometers should not be used in the microwave oven because the mercury is affected by microwave energy. However the special microwave oven thermometers are a good investment as they give a good degree of accuracy.

To insert the thermometer into meat, hold it between your thumb and forefinger, measure on the outside edge of the meat the distance to the centre on that side and keep the fingers on that measure. Move the thermometer to the centre of the top of the meat and insert it to that measured depth at an angle to avoid any bone or fat. For cookers which have a temperature probe as an integral part of the equipment, the same principle applies, but the temperature desired is selected and programmed by controls.

A special microwave thermometer with skewer to make the hole in the food into which the thermometer is inserted.

An assortment of more specialized microwave containers. From the top clockwise: a steamer/roaster, a ring mould, an open roasting dish and a muffin pan.

Metal Unless the manufacturers of a microwave cooker confirm its use, metal utensils, pots, pans, kitchen tools or any dishes with a metal content or trim *should not be used*. Metal materials do not allow microwave energy to pass through to the food; instead they deflect such energy away and in so doing cause arcing (i.e. sparking) in the oven cavity. This disturbs the carefully balanced electro-magnetic field and can lead to serious effects on the cooker's efficiency.

Frozen food should be removed from foil packs and transferred to a suitable container before heating. One small concession with which most manufacturers agree is the use of small pieces of foil to shield vulnerable areas of food during a cooking period. Further information on this use is given in Chapter 3, page 25.

Freezer to microwave Polythene freezer bags, special freezer-proof glass and thermoplastic materials can be used both for freezer storage and heating in the microwave cooker. Remove any metal ties from the bags before heating.

Special note It is advisable not to use plastic of any description for the heating of sugar and water for caramel, or for the prolonged heating of a combination of sugar and fats. Such intensity of heat can cause the material to scar and split which would be extremely hazardous as the container is handled.

COOKING OPERATIONS AND THE MICROWAVE

An assessment of the microwave cooker shows clearly that in certain areas it compares most favourably with conventional cooking, in others less so. An understanding of the capabilities of a microwave cooker will enable you to decide when to use this method and when to use the conventional method for best results. It cannot replace the conventional cooker entirely but certainly merits recognition both as a cooker in its own right and a valuable asset in helping with many preparatory tasks.

The following sections explain its capabilities and limitations.

Boiling

The time taken to boil liquids is impressively short for small quantities and these can be heated in cups, beakers and measuring jugs. The time advantages decrease as the quantity increases, but you are still able to heat any liquids in the container from which they are to be served (provided they are microwave-safe, see Chapter 4), thus eliminating the use of saucepans and cutting down on the amount of washing-up.

Steaming and Poaching

Both these methods provide classic examples of how by cooking food in its own natural juices, with minimum additives, the microwave cooker can give perfect results. The speed of cooking, retention of nutrients and excellent flavour all compare most favourably with conventional methods.

Casseroles and Stews

These both benefit from slow cooking and are only heated on Maximum (Full) power initially until the ingredients reach a high temperature, then the power level is reduced to Medium or Medium Low power, in order to control the heating and extend the cooking time.

The cheaper cuts of beef improve if they are trimmed of gristle and excess fat and tenderized either with a natural tenderizing powder, or beaten with a meat mallet or heavy flat object to break down the connective tissue. For special occasions try marinating them in red wine or cider, a bay leaf, cloves and lemon juice, store in the refrigerator for twelve to twenty-four hours and baste frequently before cooking. Neither lamb nor pork require such preparation unless it is recommended in a particular recipe.

Any container used for casseroles should be compact but yet allow sufficient capacity for stirring the ingredients. It should have a lid or

Casseroles, such as this beef and vegetable combination, are cooked first on Maximum (Full) power, then on Medium or Medium Low power.

be used with a cover, such as an inverted plate.

Casseroles actually improve in flavour if cooked one day in advance and reheated the following day.

To cook a 750 g (1½ lb) beef and vegetable casserole, the standard method would be as follows: Prepare the meat, cut into even-sized pieces and toss in seasoned flour. Cut or finely slice an onion, together with the chosen vegetables, such as carrot and celery, and make up the hot stock as required. Heat 25–50 g (1–2 oz) of fat in a casserole and when hot, add the meat and onion, stirring to ensure an even coating of fat.

Cook for approximately 10 minutes on Maximum (Full) power, stirring once during this period. Gradually add the hot stock and any herbs, stirring all the time to make a smooth liquid content. Add the vegetables and/or any other ingredients and heat for 4 minutes on Maximum (Full) power to raise the temperature again.

Switch to Medium or Medium Low power level and cook until the meat is tender. This will take approximately 1 to 1¼ hours but does to a great extent depend on the total weight content.

Do not be too liberal with seasoning, herbs or spices as they become quite pronounced in flavour with this method of cooking.

Fruits can, however, be stewed on Maximum (Full) power; as they tenderize so quickly cooked in this way they provide an excellent base for purées and sauces.

Roasting

The success of cooking joints of meat depends greatly on the selection and grade of meat. A joint of meat is still very popular with many families but it is one of the more expensive foods and therefore should be chosen carefully (see page 73).

The correct timing and power level are of utmost importance, and standing time after

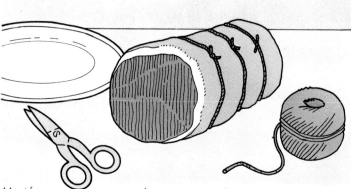

Meat for roasting is best boned, rolled and tied with string to give an even and compact shape.

cooking is essential to ensure good results. Read any such information supplied by the manufacturer of your microwave carefully and follow the recommendations which will relate to the specific output power and variable power percentage levels of your particular microwave cooker.

Pot Roasting

This method is suitable for the cooking of less expensive beef joints, e.g. brisket. As with conventional means, it requires slow cooking, so it is only suitable for cookers which have Medium/Low variable power.

Select a suitable dish with an integral lid in which there is space to turn the meat over during the cooking and to re-arrange the vegetables. Melt a little beef dripping in the dish and lightly sauté the vegetables on Maximum (Full) power.

(Alternatively both meat and vegetables can be lightly seared in a frying pan on a conventional hob before finishing the cooking by microwave.) Brush the outside of the meat with these juices and place the meat on top of the vegetables, then add approximately 150 ml ($\frac{1}{4}$ pint) of seasoned stock and herbs of your choice. Cover the dish and allow between 35–40 minutes per 450 g (1 lb) of meat on Medium Low power. Allow a standing time of 15 minutes. Remove the meat and vegetables and keep warm.

The juices can be thickened by mixing together 25 g (1 oz) flour and equal weight of butter to a thick paste. Heat the juices again until boiling and cut the paste into small pieces and gradually work into the liquid until it thickens; it can be returned to the cooker for further heating if necessary. This makes a well-flavoured gravy to serve with the meat and vegetables.

Alternatively the meat and other ingredients can be cooked in a roasting bag placed in a shallow dish. The ends of the bag must only be partially closed either with an elastic band or string, for there has to be an outlet through which a little of the steam can escape.

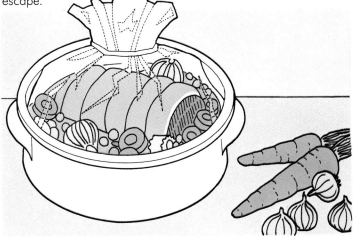

Frying

Frying is a quick conventional method of cooking food in hot fat or oil and it requires constant attention at a controlled temperature. The surface of the food is sealed as soon as it comes into contact with the hot fat and so retains its flavour.

The microwave method of cooking does not produce the same result because the temperature of fat cannot be controlled and frictional heat created in the food tends to keep it moist rather than crisp. **Therefore in its genuine form frying is neither successful nor safe to attempt in the microwave cooker.** However, you can obtain a shallow-fried effect particularly with foods that are coated with egg and breadcrumbs by heating 1–2 tablespoons of oil or butter in a shallow dish and when hot adding the food and cooking on Maximum (Full) power. As with conventional methods turn over the food during cooking.

All the ingredients for a pot roast can be put in a roasting bag, loosely closed with an elastic band and placed in a shallow dish.

Baking

Allowances must be made for the appearance of cakes, bread or pastry cooked by the microwave method as they do not have the golden brown appearance generally associated with baked products. However, careful selection of the right ingredients or decorations can help considerably to overcome this (see page 26).

Sponge-type cakes will have a good volume and very light texture and some rich fruit cakes if cooked on a Medium/Low power level will be moist, but will have a firm exterior once they have completely cooled. See also page 81 for hints on cake making. There are many

Potato croquettes can be coated in egg and breadcrumbs for a shallow-fried effect.

varieties of bread, and if a soft crust is acceptable, the cooker can and will cook a 450 g (1 lb) loaf in approximately 5–6 minutes. It can also be used for the proving of the kneaded dough. If wholemeal or similar type flour is used, the need for decoration to counteract the pale appearance of the bread is minimal (see page 27).

Some, but not all types, of pastry can be cooked. The varieties which are reasonably successful are short crust and suet crust pastry. Double crust pies are totally unsuccessful. See also pages 82 and 83.

Jam and Preserve Making

It is far less trouble to make small quantities of jams, curds, chutneys, relishes and jelly in the microwave cooker than it is by conventional methods. It is a clean method of cooking as an ovenproof glass mixing bowl can be used to which the ingredients will not stick or burn at high temperatures. Neither will the high acid content in chutney mark or stain the bowl as happens to some metal saucepans, and furthermore the kitchen itself will be free of steam during the cooking. Most conventional recipes can be adapted providing the quantities are realistic.

For microwave the quantity of fruit can be up to 1 kg (2 lb), which, plus added ingredients, will generally yield 2 kg (4 lb) of preserve, although smaller quantities can be used and will give equally successful results.

The glass storage jars can be sterilized in the microwave cooker. Half-fill the container with hot water and heat until it boils. Use oven gloves to remove the jars and carefully swirl round the liquid before emptying. Invert the jars on to absorbent kitchen paper before using. In addition to all these advantages are the excellent flavour and attractive natural colour that results from cooking by this method.

Sauce Making

Any variety of sauces can be made in the microwave, from the very simple to the exotic, and are an absolute delight to cook by the microwave method. Choose an ovenproof glass jug or bowl large enough to allow for the rapid expansion of ingredients as they cook, and to give room to stir or whisk the mixture as necessary.

Sauces are easily made in jugs but must be stirred frequently during the cooking cycle.

The operation is simple enough. For 300 ml (½ pint) of a basic white sauce, heat 25 g (1 oz) butter in the container until it is very hot, stir in 25 g (1 oz) flour and gradually add 300 ml (½ pint) milk and seasonings, stirring all the time to ensure it is free of lumps. Heat for approximately 3 minutes on Maximum (Full) power, whisking the mixture twice during the cooking period. The result is a perfectly smooth sauce and the only washing-up a jug or bowl not, as often happens, a scorched saucepan.

Even sauces which have a high egg or cream content if cooked on a low power level will not curdle. The only art is ensuring that you whisk thoroughly at intervals during the cooking.

Using the Microwave in Recipe Preparation

Time is often the deciding factor when one recipe is chosen in preference to another and it is not so much the amount of cooking time required as the length of fiddly preparation. Here the microwave cooker comes into its own as with it many of these tasks can be accomplished in seconds, with minimal use of dishes. No time is wasted in preheating the cooker and so the microwave is on hand constantly for the preparation of any meal. The microwave cooker can:

■ **Melt chocolate or confectionery bars for ice cream or dessert topping.**

Break a 100 g (4 oz) sweet bar into small pieces and place in a glass bowl or jug. Heat

A delicious ice cream topping of melted chocolate and toasted almonds is quickly prepared in a microwave cooker.

on Medium power for 2½–3 minutes, turning once halfway through.

It is advisable to heat chocolate or confectionery bars on a low power, so that you have more control over the heating. It is easy to overheat on full power.

■ **Toast coconuts and almonds for use as garnishes or decorations.**

Use a 75 g (3 oz) quantity and spread on a flat dish. Heat on Maximum (Full) power for between 5–7 minutes, stirring or rearranging several times until the required toasted colour is reached.

Do not heat smaller quantities as they will scorch.

■ **Soften fats from the refrigerator for spreading or cooking.**

To soften 225 g (8 oz) butter, heat for 1 minute on Low/Defrost power and allow to stand for 1 minute before spreading.

To soften 100 g (4 oz) of fat for cooking, heat for 1 minute on Low/Defrost power. The fat will be soft enough for creaming and beating methods.

■ **Heat small quantities of liquids.**

The microwave cooker is useful in place of a kettle in this instance. To boil 150 ml (¼ pint) water, heat for 1½–1¾ minutes on Maximum (Full) power.

To heat up the same quantity would take just under 1 minute.

■ **Caramelize sugar and water (see page 80).**

■ **Assist with the making of forcemeat or stuffings.**

Herbs can be dried in the microwave cooker (see page 69) and small quantities of vegetables, such as onions, can be pre-cooked before adding to the stuffing. For example, a small knob of butter and 50 g (2 oz) of finely chopped onions would be heated on Maximum (Full) for just 2 minutes.

■ **Make croûtons for soup.**

Melt 25 g (1 oz) of butter in a glass bowl for 1 minute. Toss in 50 g (2 oz) of cubed bread and

Croûtons made in the microwave cooker make a quick and tasty garnish for soup.

stir to ensure even coating. Heat for 1 minute on Maximum (Full) power, stir thoroughly and heat for a further minute. Cover with a plate and allow to stand for 2 minutes before serving.

■ **Make savoury breadcrumb toppings.**
Melt 25 g (a scant 1 oz) of butter for approximately 1 minute. Stir in the breadcrumbs and seasonings. Heat for 2 minutes on Maximum (Full) power, stirring three or four times during this period. Spread out on to a paper towel and allow to cool.

■ **Make biscuit bases (see page 80).**
■ **Heat items that have cooled before serving.**
■ **Defrost frozen food for cookery preparation.**

In fact, a microwave cooker has many uses in the preparation and serving of food at any mealtime.

Reheating

The microwave cooker is incomparably the safest and most efficient way to reheat cooked foods. With few exceptions, Maximum (Full) power is used for reheating and the very high internal temperatures reached reduce many of the health risks associated with the slower warming methods. This manifold convenience will give excellent results provided that a few simple instructions are followed:

■ As with cooking, most foods once they are reheated also require a brief standing time in order to equalize the heat before they are served.

■ Very small portions of food between 50–75 g (2–3 oz) need only a few seconds to reheat and such low denominations are not always shown on 'timer' calibrations. You can count mentally but as a precaution against the food being cooked again (rather than just reheated) and so altering the texture, it is advisable to reduce the power level to Defrost control and slightly lengthen the time accordingly.

■ It is inadvisable to heat or cook very small amounts in the microwave cooker as the microwave energy is too powerful, but just softening, say 25 g (1 oz) of butter is permissible as it is merely changing the texture, not cooking in the truest sense.

The following sections give hints on reheating plate meals, cooked pastries, bread and varieties of canned foods.

Plate meals Arrange the foods on the plates with the thicker or denser parts to the outer edges and the thinner, more delicate foods towards the centre. Large potatoes should be cut into even-shaped pieces and the meal should be so arranged that it does not exceed 4–5 cm (1½–2 inches) in height. Unless a pastry item is part of the meal, cover the plate with cling film to keep the food moist, but pierce it lightly to prevent 'ballooning' (see page 93).

REHEATING CONVENIENCE FOODS

Note: Canned foods – transfer all food from cans to a suitable microwave-safe container

Food	Quantity	Method
Baked beans	220 g (7¾ oz) 425 g (15 oz)	Place in shallow dish and cover
Custard & milk puddings	440 g (15½ oz)	Place in serving jug or bowl
Macaroni cheese	425 g (15 oz)	Place in bowl or serving plate and cover
Meat balls in sauce	400 g (14 oz)	Place in shallow dish and cover
Peas/sweetcorn/ sliced carrots etc.	425 g (15 oz)	Place in bowl and cover
Soup	1 serving 2 servings	Pour into mug or soup bowl
Spaghetti in tomato sauce	440 g (15½ oz)	Place in bowl and cover
Sponge pudding	300 g (11 oz)	Place on serving dish, cover with small bowl
Steak & kidney pudding	425 g (15 oz)	Place in serving dish and cover with small bowl
Tomatoes	400 g (14 oz)	Place in bowl and cover

REHEATING REFRIGERATED FOODS

Note: Timings are approximate to allow for variations in the temperature of the refrigerator

Food	Quantity	Method
Baked apple, cooked	1 serving 2 servings	Place on serving plate
Butter	250 g (½ lb)	To soften for spreading. Remove wrapper and place in dish
Chicken portion, cooked	1 weighing approx 250 g (8 oz)	Place thinner area towards centre of plate, cover loosely
Pasta, cooked	1 serving 2 servings 4 servings	Dot with butter or margarine and loosely cover the serving dish
Plated meal, cooked	350–450 g (12–16 oz)	Arrange thinner foods to centre of plate, cover with cling film (unless pastry is included) and pierce the top
Potatoes, whole, cooked	1 serving 2 servings	Place in shallow dish, cut into uniform size. Dot with butter or margarine
Rice, cooked	1 serving 2 servings 4 servings	Loosely cover the serving dish
Sausages, cooked	2 4	Place on serving dish

Time on Maximum (Full) power	Special points
1$\frac{1}{2}$ minutes 3–3$\frac{1}{2}$ minutes	Stir once during cooking
2$\frac{1}{2}$–3 minutes	Stir once during cooking
4–4$\frac{1}{2}$ minutes	Stir twice during cooking
4–4$\frac{1}{2}$ minutes	Stir once during cooking
3$\frac{1}{2}$–4 minutes	Stir once during cooking
2–2$\frac{1}{2}$ minutes 4–5 minutes	Stir once during cooking
3–3$\frac{1}{2}$ minutes	Stir once during cooking
1$\frac{1}{2}$ minutes	Allow to stand 2 minutes before serving
4–4$\frac{1}{2}$ minutes	Allow to stand 4–5 minutes before serving
3$\frac{1}{2}$–4 minutes	Stir once during cooking

Power level and time	Special points
1 minute on Maximum (Full) 1$\frac{1}{2}$–2 minutes on Maximum (Full)	Allow to stand for 3 minutes before serving
1 minute on Defrost	
2$\frac{1}{2}$ minutes on Maximum (Full)	Allow to stand for 2 minutes before serving
1–1$\frac{1}{2}$ minutes on Maximum (Full) 1$\frac{1}{2}$–2 minutes on Maximum (Full) 2$\frac{1}{2}$–3$\frac{1}{2}$ minutes on Maximum (Full)	Fork stir halfway through the cooking.
3–4$\frac{1}{2}$ minutes on Maximum (Full)	Timing relates to density and weight. Allow to stand for 2 minutes before serving.
1–1$\frac{1}{2}$ minutes on Maximum (Full) 2–2$\frac{1}{2}$ minutes on Maximum (Full)	Add seasoning if required
$\frac{1}{2}$–1 minute on Maximum (Full) 1–2 minutes on Maximum (Full) 2$\frac{1}{2}$–3$\frac{1}{2}$ minutes on Maximum (Full)	Fork stir halfway through the cooking
1–1$\frac{1}{2}$ minutes on Defrost 2–3 minutes on Defrost	Allow to stand for 2 minutes before serving

REHEATING PREPARED BAKERY ITEMS

Note: Transfer any food from foil trays to a suitable microwave-safe container before heating. The following times apply to food at room temperature

Food	Quantity	Method
Christmas pudding	450 g (1 lb) or 1 kg (2 lb)	Remove any wrapping, place in suitable basin, cover with cling film and pierce the top
	1 portion only	Place on plate
Cornish pasty	1	Place on paper towel
	2	
Family size meat pie	450 g (1 lb) approx.	Place on serving dish
Individual fruit pie	1	Place on serving plate
Individual meat pie	1	Place on paper towel
Mince pies	1	Place on paper towel
	4	
Pizza	large	Place on serving plate
	1 portion	
Quiche	18 cm (7 inches) in diameter	Place on serving dish and prick centre with fork
Sausage rolls	4	Place on paper towel

Family dishes Many dishes can be prepared a few hours ahead of time and some even made the day before, then reheated. Always allow a little extra time if they are taken straight from the refrigerator.

Dense foods, such as shepherd's, cottage, or fish pie, which have a good potato topping, should be lightly forked up on the top to form small peaks.

Layered pasta dishes, such as lasagne, or other similar combined recipes can be pierced through in several places with a small, sharp-pointed knife.

If necessary, dishes can be lightly browned under the conventional grill, either before or after reheating.

Piercing or forking helps the microwave energy to penetrate through to the centre of the food. The dishes need only to be loosely covered with cling film or paper towels.

Soups Wherever possible heat individual portions in soup bowls to speed the action, rather than in soup plates which spread the contents

Power level and time	Special points
2½–3 minutes on Maximum (Full) 4–5 minutes on Maximum (Full) 1 minute on Defrost	Allow to stand for 4 minutes before inverting on to serving dish. Allow to stand for 5 minutes before inverting on to serving dish.
1½–2 minutes on Defrost 3½–4 minutes on Defrost	Allow to stand for 2 minutes
3 minutes on Maximum (Full) 3 minutes on Defrost	Allow to stand for 4 minutes
1–1½ minutes on Defrost	Allow to stand for 2 minutes
1–2 minutes on Defrost	Allow to stand for 2 minutes
30 seconds on Defrost 1–1½ minutes on Defrost	Allow to stand for 1– 2 minutes before serving
4–5 minutes on Maximum (Full) 1–1½ minutes on Maximum (Full)	Place under medium grill briefly to finish
5 minutes on Defrost	Allow to stand for 3 minutes before serving
1½ minutes on Defrost	Allow to stand for 2 minutes

over a wider area. Similarly if heating several servings in one container, use a compact shape, deep enough to allow for stirring rather than a wide shallow container.

Soups need to be stirred once during the heating period and again after they have been taken from the cooker.

Vegetables Any leftover vegetables can be reheated and providing they were not over-cooked initially, will retain good flavour and fresh appearance. Sprinkle a little water over the vegetables and cover them with a lid or cling film. If large quantities are reheated they will need to be rearranged or stirred during the process. Seasoning and butter can be added after the reheating if required.

Casseroles and stews should be covered for reheating with a lid or cling film. The contents should be rearranged and stirred during the heating. How often you do this is related to the volume of food: the greater the quantity, the more frequently it is stirred.

Rice and pasta To try to reheat rice and pasta by conventional means is never totally suc-cessful as invariably they dry out and lose their flavour. Reheating these by microwave, however, will give a fresh-cooked flavour and texture. Cover the dish with cling film or a lid to retain natural moisture and lightly fork half-way through the heating cycle.

Pastry Pastry products are best heated on a paper towel, which will absorb some of the excess moisture from the base.

Double crust pastry tends to go limp after heating but this can be overcome by briefly crisping the surface under a preheated conventional grill.

Small pastry items with a high sugar content,

Pasta dishes remain moist and delicious when reheated in a microwave cooker.

such as mince pies or individual fruit pies, should be reheated on Defrost power to control the rapid increase in temperature of the filling.

Pizzas will reheat, but the best results are obtained by using a preheated microwave browning dish.

Bread Rolls should be loosely wrapped in a napkin or paper towel, and filled rolls, such as hamburgers, can be placed on a paper napkin for reheating, then served as a hand snack.

Canned food Any variety of canned foods may be reheated successfully provided the contents are removed from the can and emptied into a suitable serving dish. Any foods which are packed in a foil container should be removed and inverted on to a microwave-safe serving dish.

Cover sponge puddings with a small basin and reheat on Defrost power; reheat meat puddings on Maximum (Full) power, in the same manner or cover with a loose wrapping of greaseproof paper.

Blanching Before Freezing

Small quantities of freshly picked vegetables can be blanched in a microwave cooker. This is particularly advantageous to people who grow their own vegetables, as they can pick in small quantities when the vegetables are at the peak of perfection.

▓ The vegetables should be washed or scrubbed, trimmed and diced to a uniform size, just as you would for cooking.

▓ For 450 g (1 lb) vegetables, rinse them and place in a deep dish with 3 tablespoons water. Stir or arrange, so that the water evenly coats the vegetables, then cover and heat

for 3–5 minutes depending on the density of the vegetables. Stir the vegetables halfway through cooking. Immerse the vegetables in ice cold water, then drain, pat dry, pack and freeze.

▓ For 225 g (½ lb) vegetables, rinse the vegetables in the same way, making sure that a small degree of water still adheres to them. Place in a small freezer bag and loosely secure with a rubber band. Heat for 1½–2 minutes, shaking the bag halfway through. The rinsing water creates the steam for blanching. Remove from the oven and immerse the bag in ice cold water keeping the sealed end just above the level of the water. This will chill the vegetables and expel the air in the bag at the same time, automatically creating a vacuum pack for the freezer. Dry the outside of the bag, seal and freeze in the normal manner.

Vegetables in 225 g (½ lb) amounts can be blanched in the freezer bag loosely closed, then plunged into cold water before tightly securing.

Defrosting Foods

The many different foods stored in a freezer include raw foods, such as meat, poultry, fish, fruit and frozen vegetables, processed, convenience foods and home-made dishes cooked either by conventional or microwave methods. These are packed into varying weights, shapes and containers and consequently there are variations in the techniques

GUIDE TO DEFROSTING FRUITS

Fruit	Quantity	Method
Apples, free-flow slices	225 g (8 oz) 450 g (1 lb)	Turn contents into shallow dish and cover
Blackberries	225 g (8 oz) 450 g (1 lb)	Turn contents into shallow dish Do not cover
Cherries	225 g (8 oz) 450 g (1 lb)	Turn contents into shallow dish and cover
Damsons	225 g (8 oz) 450 g (1 lb)	Turn contents into shallow dish and cover
Fruit juice concentrate	175 g (6 oz)	Remove lid. Tip block into jug
Fruit salad, dry sugar pack	225 g (8 oz) 450 g (1 lb)	Turn contents into shallow dish and cover
Gooseberries	225 g (8 oz) 450 g (1 lb)	Turn contents into shallow dish and cover
Greengages	225 g (8 oz) 450 g (1 lb)	Turn contents into shallow dish and cover
Peach halves in syrup	225 g (8 oz) 450 g (1 lb)	Turn contents into shallow dish and cover
Plums	225 g (8 oz) 450 g (1 lb)	Turn contents into shallow dish and cover
Raspberries	225 g (8 oz) 450 g (1 lb)	Turn contents into shallow dish Do not cover
Rhubarb	225 g (8 oz) 450 g (1 lb)	Turn contents into shallow dish and cover
Strawberries	225 g (8 oz) 450 g (1 lb)	Turn contents into shallow dish. Do not cover

used for successful defrosting. The following sections take the popular frozen foods category by category. The timings are based on a microwave cooker with a 700 watt output power and a defrost power level of approximately 220 watts. For models with a lower output power, timings would have to be slightly extended. There are a few simple rules, which are common to defrosting of all foods.

■ Remove any food from foil or metal containers and transfer to a microwave-safe dish of the same size where possible.

■ Remove any metal ties.

Pierce any plastic pouches, and if the food inside is being cooked, not simply defrosted, flex the pouch during the cooking to help even out the heat distribution.

Open all cartons and remove any lids before defrosting liquids.

■ If small areas of food of the dense variety,

Time on Defrost power	Special points
3–3½ minutes 5–6 minutes	Rearrange fruit during defrosting. Stand for 5–6 minutes.
3½–4 minutes 5–6 minutes	Rearrange fruit during defrosting. Stand for 8 minutes. Stand for 8–10 minutes.
4–5 minutes 6½–7 minutes	Rearrange fruit during defrosting. Stand for 8 minutes.
4–5 minutes 6½–7 minutes	Rearrange fruit during defrosting. Stand for 8 minutes.
1½ minutes	Break up block halfway through. Dilute with cold water and serve.
3–3½ minutes 5–6 minutes	Rearrange fruit during defrosting. Stand for 8–10 minutes.
4½–5 minutes 7–8 minutes	Rearrange fruit during defrosting. Stand for 5–7 minutes.
5–6 minutes 8–9 minutes	Rearrange fruit during defrosting. Stand for 8–10 minutes.
6–7 minutes 9–10 minutes	Separate halves during defrosting and rearrange. Stand for 8–10 minutes.
5–6 minutes 8–9 minutes	Rearrange fruit during defrosting. Stand for 8–10 minutes.
3½–4 minutes 5–6 minutes	Rearrange fruit during defrosting. Stand for 5–6 minutes.
4–5 minutes 6½–7 minutes	Rearrange fruit during defrosting. Stand for 2–5 minutes.
3½–4 minutes 5–6 minutes	Rearrange fruit during defrosting. Stand for 5–6 minutes.

i.e. meat and poultry, start to feel appreciably warm, shield such areas with small pieces of foil kept in place with wooden cocktail sticks (see page 28).

If a great amount of moisture is released during defrosting, remove this as it will rapidly continue to attract microwave energy from the frozen block.

Frozen fruits Frozen fruits required for cold desserts should be partially defrosted to give the best results and the standing period will complete the thawing process. If they receive too much microwave energy they tend to soften and collapse.

Frozen fruits can also be cooked straight from the freezer on Maximum (Full) power if they need to be served hot, and take approximately the same time as the defrost recommendations but should be stirred quite frequently during cooking. The high proportion of natural sugar results in very quick cooking, and it is advisable to remove them from the cooker when they are hot but still quite whole, for they can very quickly turn to pulp.

Very soft fruits do not require to be covered.

Vegetables Frozen raw vegetables are cooked on Maximum (Full) power as they do not require a defrost period.

As they have a high moisture content very little, if any, liquid needs to be added before cooking.

Small varieties of vegetables can be

GUIDE TO FROZEN VEGETABLE COOKING

Vegetable	Quantity	Container/Method
Asparagus	225 g (8 oz)	Covered shallow dish. Add 2 tablespoons water.
Beans Broad	225 g (8 oz)	Covered shallow dish. Add 2 tablespoons water.
French	225 g (8 oz)	Covered shallow dish. Add 3 tablespoons water.
Runner	225 g (8 oz)	Covered shallow dish. Add 3 tablespoons water.
Broccoli	225 g (8 oz)	Covered shallow dish. Add 2 tablespoons water.
Brussels sprouts	225 g (8 oz)	Covered shallow dish. Add 4 tablespoons water.
Cauliflower florets	225 g (8 oz)	Covered shallow dish. Add 4 tablespoons water.
Carrots	225 g (8 oz) whole	Covered shallow dish. Add 2 tablespoons water.
Corn-on-the-cob	2 ears	Wrap in buttered greaseproof paper.
Courgettes	225 g (8 oz)	Covered shallow dish. Add 2 tablespoons water.
Leaf spinach	225 g (8 oz)	Covered shallow dish.
Mixed vegetables	225 g (8 oz)	Cook in pouch and pierce top. Flex pouch during cooking.
Onions, sliced	225 g (8 oz)	Covered shallow dish.
Peas	225 g (8 oz)	Cook in pouch and pierce top. Flex pouch during cooking.
Stewpack	225 g (8 oz)	Cook in pouch and pierce top. Flex pouch during cooking.
Sweetcorn	225 g (8 oz)	Cook in pouch and pierce top. Flex pouch during cooking.

cooked in their plastic pouches. Pierce the top and flex the pouch during cooking as mentioned above.

■ All vegetables should be covered and stirred halfway through the cooking.

Frozen fish To get the best results from microwave cooking, fish should first be defrosted. This is a fairly quick process and the fish should be removed from the oven while still cold yet pliable. Use the minimum defrost period to start with. This will prevent thinner areas from beginning to cook with the danger than they will become tough during the actual cooking process. See chart on page 55 for timings.

■ Always consider the shape and thickness of the pack, as it will affect timings necessary for successful defrosting.

■ Where possible defrost fish in the commercially packed plastic wrapping, or loosely cover any fish during this sequence.

■ Block frozen fish fillets should be turned over during an initial defrosting period. Separate the fillets as soon as possible and arrange them in a single layer before continuing the defrosting. Rinse under running cold water if any ice crystals remain.

■ Arrange a whole fish in a suitably-sized dish and defrost for half the suggested time, then turn it over and continue defrosting. Dependent on thickness, it may be necessary

Cooking time
6–7 minutes +3 minutes standing
7–8 minutes +3 minutes standing
6–7 minutes +2 minutes standing
5–6 minutes +2 minutes standing
6–7 minutes +2 minutes standing
7–8 minutes +3 minutes standing
6–7 minutes +3 minutes standing
6–7 minutes +3 minutes standing
6–7 minutes +2 minutes standing
4–5 minutes +2 minutes standing
5–6 minutes +2 minutes standing
5–6 minutes +2 minutes standing
3–4 minutes
4–5 minutes +2 minutes standing
6–7 minutes +2 minutes standing
4–5 minutes +2 minutes standing

to give the dish a half turn or cover the thin end with a strip of aluminium foil (see page 28). Rinse the cavity of the fish after the defrosting period and leave aside to complete the standing time.

▓ Spread individually frozen shellfish on a plate in a single layer and rearrange halfway through defrosting.

▓ Block frozen shellfish will start to defrost at the outer edges, just loosen the affected shellfish and remove them. Turn the block over. Try to gently break the block with a fork, or separate individual portions and continue with the defrosting. Allow to stand to defrost completely.

▓ Frozen breadcrumbed fish can be brushed with a little melted butter and cooked, on a preheated browning dish. This will slightly crisp the surface.

Frozen poultry To defrost whole chickens, ducks and game, refer to the chart and calculate the total time for defrosting by multiplying the minutes per 450 g (1 lb) by the total weight of the bird. Added to this, allowance must be made for the recommended standing periods which are necessary to obtain an even temperature throughout the bird before cooking. Timings are approximate only to allow for variations in the density of the poultry and in the commercial method of freezing. Defrosting is always

GUIDE TO DEFROSTING POULTRY AND GAME

Poultry/Game	Time in minutes per 450 g (1 lb) on Defrost power	Standing time after defrosting
Chicken, whole	7–8 minutes	20–25 minutes
Chicken pieces	7–8 minutes	8–10 minutes
Duck, whole	7–8 minutes	25–30 minutes
Grouse	5–6 minutes	15–20 minutes
Partridge	5–6 minutes	15–20 minutes
Pheasant	5–6 minutes	15–20 minutes
Pigeon	4–5 minutes	10–15 minutes
Rabbit, joints boneless cubes block frozen	7–8 minutes 8–9 minutes	8–10 minutes 10–15 minutes
Turkey, whole Up to 3½ kg (7 lb) Over 3½ kg (7 lb) and up to 4½ kg (10 lb)	8–9 minutes 10–11 minutes	30 minutes 30–40 minutes

GUIDE TO DEFROSTING MEAT – SMALLER CUTS

Type and weight of meat	Time on Defrost power	Standing time	Special points
Bacon 225 g (8 oz)	3–4 minutes	5 minutes	Separate rashers during defrosting.
Cubed meat Stewing/Braising 450 g (1 lb)	8–9 minutes	8–10 minutes	Separate pieces of meat during defrosting.
Kidneys 450 g (1 lb)	4–5 minutes		Separate kidneys and leave to defrost naturally.
Lamb chops 2 × 100 g (4 oz)	4–5 minutes	5–6 minutes	Separate chops during defrosting.
Liver 450 g (1 lb)	4–5 minutes		Separate slices and leave to defrost naturally.
Minced meat 450 g (1 lb)	8–9 minutes	8–10 minutes	Break up with a fork twice during defrosting. Remove any thawed meat.
Sausages 450 g (1 lb)	5–6 minutes	8–10 minutes	Separate and rearrange halfway through defrosting.
Steak Individual thick	3–4 minutes		Leave to defrost naturally.
Individual thin	2–3 minutes		Leave to defrost naturally.

carried out on the Defrost power level and it helps if you check occasionally for warm spots, which can occur on the thinner parts, such as the wing tips and tail end (see page 56).

■ The giblets can be just loosened at the end of the defrosting period by easing the

GUIDE TO DEFROSTING AND COOKING FISH

Fish	Quantity	Time on Defrost power	Standing time
Crabmeat	225 g (8 oz)	6–7 minutes	5 minutes
Fish fillets, Cod, Plaice, Haddock, etc.	450 g (1 lb)	7–8 minutes	5 minutes
Fish steak	175 g (6 oz)	2–3 minutes	3 minutes
Fish steaks	2 × 175 g (6 oz)	4–5 minutes	5 minutes
Mackerel	2 × 350 g (12 oz)	10–12 minutes	8 minutes
Prawns, Scampi	100 g (4 oz) 450 g (1 lb)	2–2½ minutes 6–7 minutes	3 minutes 5 minutes
Scallops	450 g (1 lb)	8–9 minutes	5 minutes
Trout, Herring	1 × 1¼ kg (3 lb)	15–16 minutes	10 minutes
Whole fish, gutted	2 × 225 g (8 oz)	8–9 minutes	8 minutes

GUIDE TO DEFROSTING MEAT – JOINTS

Meat	Time per 450 g (1 lb) on Defrost power	Total standing time	Special points
Beef, boned & rolled	7–8 minutes	20–30 minutes	Turn over and on sides during defrosting.
Beef, joints on bone	9–10 minutes	30–40 minutes	Cover bone end with foil* during defrosting and turn over.
Lamb, leg	8–9 minutes	15–20 minutes	Cover knuckle end of joint with foil* halfway through defrosting and turn over.
Lamb, shoulder	6–7 minutes	15–20 minutes	Foreleg may need covering with foil* during defrosting. Turn over.
Pork, top fillet of leg	7–8 minutes	30–40 minutes	Turn over during defrosting.
Veal, leg	7–8 minutes	15–20 minutes	Cover knuckle end of joint halfway through defrosting. Turn over.
Veal, shoulder	6–7 minutes	15–20 minutes	If any foreleg, cover with foil* halfway through defrosting and turn over.

* See page 28 for use of small pieces of foil.

legs. The cavity should be rinsed with cold running water and the giblets removed. The inside should feel very cold but not frozen.

■ A final standing period of 20 minutes after defrosting is necessary to ensure the bird is an even temperature throughout before it is cooked.

Remove the metal ties from the plastic wrapping and place the chicken breast-side down in a glass roasting dish. Defrost for one third of the total time. Remove the wrapper. Check for warm spots and shield these with small pieces of aluminium foil (see page 28) secured with a cocktail stick if necessary. Allow to stand 3 minutes. Turn the chicken breast-side up and defrost for a further third of the total time. Check for warm spots and shield if necessary. Allow to stand for 3 minutes. Defrost for the remaining period.

■ A turkey up to 4½kg (10lb) in weight can be defrosted in the microwave. Estimate the total time necessary from the chart details given on page 54 and divide this into quarter periods.

■ Remove any metal ties but keep wrapped and place the turkey, breast-side down in a shallow dish. Defrost for a quarter of the total time. Remove the wrapper, then allow to stand for 10 minutes.

■ Use small strips of foil to shield any areas which feel slightly warm (see page 28), then turn the turkey breast-side up. Defrost for a quarter of the total time. Allow to stand for 10 minutes. Check for warm spots, shielding them and the wing tips as before.

■ Turn the turkey over and rotate the dish so that the turkey legs point to the opposite side of the oven. Defrost for a quarter of the total cooking time. Allow to stand for a further 10 minutes.

■ Turn the turkey over and defrost for the remaining time. Spread the legs and wings from the body, loosen giblets and rinse the cavity in cold water. Allow a final standing of approximately 30 minutes or until the temperature is even throughout.

■ When defrosting portions which have been individually frozen, place them in a shallow dish, with the meatier parts to the outside and loosely cover. If they are block frozen, wrap them in greaseproof paper and defrost in three stages. After the first stage you should be able to separate the joints, so they can continue defrosting in a single layer during the second stage, and they should then be turned over for the third stage. A final standing period of 8–10 minutes is recommended before cooking.

Frozen meat

The speed and convenience of defrosting meat in the microwave can add a greater variety of meals to your weekly menu. For this section of microwave usage there are so many variables that it really is worthwhile making notes for your own reference, especially if you purchase your meat from the same supplier and the packing is always of a regular standard.

To defrost meat joints refer to the chart details given on page 54 and multiply the recommended time by the weight. For example a 1½ kg (3 lb) joint of pork at 7–8 minutes to the 450 g (1 lb) would take 21–24 minutes to defrost.

To ensure an even result it is better if this total defrosting time is carried out in two or three stages interspersed with standing periods of a few minutes duration, which gradually induces heat equalization throughout the joint. If the standing periods are not included there is a tendency for parts of the outer surfaces to begin to cook while the centre remains partially frozen. The final standing time is the time needed to relax the meat after the defrosting sequence.

To ensure even cooking you must have an even temperature throughout the meat to start with and that is why the final standing time is also of importance.

If you do find warm spots occurring on the outer surfaces, just shield them with a little aluminium foil (see page 28), which can be held in place with a wooden cocktail stick. Any large bone areas, for example on a rib of beef, also require shielding for at least half of the defrosting cycle.

When defrosting a block of small pieces or cubes of meat, remove the outer pieces once they have started to defrost and place them in a shallow dish, gradually adding the remainder of the meat as it defrosts enough to be separated.

Pasta, rice and pulses

Cooked rice and pasta can be frozen and heated in the microwave oven with quite acceptable results. Details of how to cook pasta, rice and pulses are given on pages 75, 76 and 78 and there is a chart of timings on page 77.

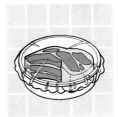

To defrost cuts such as steaks, chops, etc., remove as much wrapping as possible from the meat and, if they are block frozen, try to separate out the individual pieces with a knife. Place the thinner portions towards the centre of the dish and cover. If you cannot separate them initially use a small amount of defrost energy until that is possible. Turn over during defrosting cycle.

Meat joints should be covered during defrosting to retain moisture and they should be turned over at least once during the process to ensure even absorption of microwave energy.

To defrost minced meat and sausage meat, defrost for a couple of minutes, loosen any of the softened meat and set aside. Break the remainder down with a fork, rearrange in the dish and complete the defrosting time.

GUIDE TO DEFROSTING BAKERY ITEMS

Food	Quantity	Method
Bread		
Large sliced loaf	1	Leave in wrap, remove tie tags
Large loaf, unwrapped	1	Place on oven b(on paper towel
Small loaf, unwrapped	1	Place on oven b(on paper towel
Bread rolls	2	Wrap in paper towel
Pitta bread	2	Place on paper towel
Cakes		
Light fruit cake	700 g (1½ lb) approx	Place on paper doily
Individual small cakes and buns	6	Arrange in ring pattern on paper
Cream-filled sponge	18 cm (7 inches) diameter approx.	Place on paper doily
Cheesecake	25 cm (10 inches) diameter approx.	Place on serving plate
Pastry		
Flans*	18 cm (7 inches) diameter approx.	Place on paper towel
Flaky pastry	200 g (7½ oz)	Leave in wrapping
	375 g (13 oz)	Leave in wrapping
Quiche Lorraine*	18 cm (7 inches) diameter approx.	Place on paper towel
Sausage rolls*	4	Place on paper towel
Shortcrust pastry	200 g (7½ oz)	Leave in wrapping
	375 g (13 oz)	Leave in wrapping

* These three items will require a brief heating period following the defrost time if they are to be served hot. Flaky pastry would not remain crisp on further heating.

For example: To heat 225 g (8 oz) cooked weight of frozen pasta, place in a shallow dish and cover. Heat for 3 minutes on Defrost power. Stand for 2 minutes and separate the pieces, using a fork. Dot with a little butter. Heat for 3 minutes on Maximum (Full) power but toss the pasta in the dish halfway through the sequence.

To heat 100 g (4 oz) cooked weight of frozen rice, place in a shallow dish and cover. Heat for 1½ minutes on Defrost power. Stand for 2 minutes and separate the rice with a fork. Heat for 1–1½ minutes on Maximum (Full) power and fluff up with a fork before serving. Pulses cooked conventionally and stored in a refrigerator or deep freeze will reheat quite satisfactorily. From the frozen state, cover and heat on Defrost or Medium power first,

Time on Defrost power	Standing time
3 minutes, stand for 3 minutes, then 3 minutes	7–8 minutes
4 minutes, stand for 4 minutes, then 3 minutes	8–10 minutes
2 minutes, stand for 3 minutes, then 2–3 minutes	5 minutes
1–$1\frac{1}{2}$ minutes	2–3 minutes
1–$1\frac{1}{2}$ minutes	3–4 minutes
$2\frac{1}{2}$ minutes, stand for 2 minutes, then 2 minutes	10 minutes
2–$2\frac{1}{2}$ minutes	4 minutes
1–$1\frac{1}{2}$ minutes	Allow to defrost naturally
2–$2\frac{1}{2}$ minutes, stand for 5 minutes, then $1\frac{1}{2}$–2 minutes	Allow to defrost naturally
4–5 minutes	3–4 minutes
$1\frac{1}{2}$–2 minutes	Allow to defrost naturally
$1\frac{1}{2}$–2 minutes	Allow to defrost naturally
4–5 minutes	3–4 minutes
1–$1\frac{1}{2}$ minutes	2 minutes
$1\frac{1}{2}$–2 minutes	Allow to defrost naturally
$2\frac{1}{2}$–3 minutes	Allow to defrost naturally

then as the heat starts to create a little moisture, stir gently and continue to heat on Maximum (Full) power.

Frozen bakery products *Uncooked* frozen pastry items are not suitable for microwave methods and are best cooked in the conventional manner. However, many ***cooked*** bakery items stored in the freezer can be successfully defrosted and this method can prove useful for many occasions.

▪ Large double crust pies are an exception and are best reheated from frozen by conventional methods.

▪ If the pastry tends to go limp after defrosting, placing it under a conventional grill for a brief period will give it a crisper texture.

▪ Breads vary in texture and the heavier,

GUIDE TO DEFROSTING READY-PREPARED FROZEN FOODS

Food	Quantity	Method	Time on Defrost power
Baked sponge with fruit base	Transfer to suitable dish and loosely cover, thaw and heat in one cycle		
Beefburgers	4	Heat browning dish for 5 minutes, coat with oil.	$3\frac{1}{2}$–4 minutes
Fish fingers	6	Heat browning dish for 4 minutes, lightly coat fish fingers with melted butter.	4–$4\frac{1}{2}$ minutes
Individual boil-in-the-bag entrées	225 g (8 oz)	Slit bag and place on serving plate	5 minutes, stand for 2 minutes
Lasagne/ Moussaka	450 g (1 lb) approx.	Transfer to serving dish and cover	6 minutes, stand for 3 minutes, then 6 minutes
Meat casserole	700 g ($1\frac{1}{2}$ lb)	Place in shallow dish and cover	6 minutes, break up with fork, stand for 3 minutes, then 6 minutes
Pizza	Family size	Heat browning dish for 5 minutes, coat with oil and place pizza on dish	$4\frac{1}{2}$–5 minutes
Plate meal	350 g (12 oz) approx.	Cover with cling film, pierce the top.	4 minutes, stand for 4 minutes, then 4 minutes
Seafood pasta	400 g (14 oz)	Transfer to serving dish and cover	9 minutes, stand for 5 minutes
Shepherd's pie	450 g (1 lb) approx.	Transfer to serving dish	5 minutes, stand for 3 minutes, then 5 minutes

steam-baked varieties will take longer to defrost than lighter textures, such as Vienna or French bread.

■ **Sliced loaves** may be left in their wrapping with the ties removed when defrosting. Allowing a standing period halfway through will equalize the heat and prevent a large loaf from drying out at the edges.

■ **Bread slices** should be wrapped in paper towels to defrost.

■ Light pastries and cakes can be placed on paper towels, which will absorb any excess of moisture.

■ **Gâteaux** with a very high cream content

Cooking time on Maximum (Full) power	Special points
6–8 minutes	Time varies according to weight. Stand for 5 minutes after heating.
–	Turn over halfway through cooking. Allow to stand 2 minutes before serving.
–	Turn over halfway through cooking.
1½–2 minutes	Empty contents from bag on to serving plate after cooking cycle.
7–8 minutes	After first defrosting period, insert sharp knife into centre of the food. Allow to stand 3 minutes after final cooking.
5–7 minutes	Re-arrange meat portions after defrosting. Stir twice during cooking cycle.
–	Allow to stand 2 minutes.
–	Base of plate will indicate temperature.
6–7 minutes	Break up with fork halfway through defrost cycle. Stir halfway through cooking cycle. Allow to stand 3 minutes before serving.
5–6 minutes	Insert tines of fork through the potato before the final cooking. Allow to stand 3 minutes before serving.

should be briefly defrosted on the lowest possible setting for just 1½–2 minutes to start off the thawing process. After this leave them to thaw naturally.

Frozen convenience foods The above recommendations for a selection of ready-prepared frozen foods are approximations only to allow for the method of freezing, the storage temperature and the shape in which they are frozen when packed. Quantities are based on average product sizes. As most of these are frozen in foil packs do remember to transfer to the serving dish of similar size before defrosting.

THE MICROWAVE AND HEALTHY EATING

For most of us, eating is one of life's pleasures, and during recent years, the link between diet and health has become a much discussed subject. The medical profession emphasizes the many health risks associated with being overweight, and many people seeking a positive approach to reducing their weight, consult their own doctor who in turn prescribes a diet or recommends one which is most suitable. Others join one of the increasing number of slimming clubs and groups, or rely on comprehensive information given through the media. In addition to following weight-reducing diets, more and more people are becoming vegetarian, or are turning to wholefood diets in order to maintain a healthy existence.

Our whole attitude to eating is gradually changing and people seek a diet which suits the life they lead and which is relatively easy to keep to, so that they develop a new pattern of eating which becomes permanent: then they are less likely to put weight back on again.

Most diets recommend that food should be as free of fat as possible, of a low calorific content, but balanced by a proportionate amount of protein as this will compensate for the reduction in fat and carbohydrates. Very good examples of such foods are to be found in fish and poultry. The microwave method of cooking does not require added fat as the food cooks in its own natural juices, which is a bonus for the weight conscious, and important for those on a low cholesteral diet. Vegetables and fruit are important to a healthy diet as they not only contain essential minerals and vitamins, but also supply the fibre that is a necessary aid to a good digestion. Very little liquid, if any, is needed to cook these foods so a high percentage of nutrients are retained.

Starting a diet is not so difficult, sticking to a diet can be, for food must always look and taste good and be sufficiently varied to prevent diet boredom.

A microwave cooker is a valuable aid for such tasks, it is a clean, efficient way of preparing delicious foods. Its versatility will provide an extensive selection of suitable recipes from which the individual or the whole family will benefit.

Vegetables

Vegetables have many uses in a healthy diet as they are low-calorie and fat-free, and, whether fresh or frozen, cooked by microwave they retain their colour and crispness. The flavour is excellent, so the need for salt is reduced, but for a contrasting flavour after cooking try tossing in a knob of low-fat spread and freshly chopped herbs.

Nourishing soups can be made by combining 1 litre (1¼ pints) of hot stock with small diced vegetables of choice. Microwave until the vegetables are just cooked and still firm and serve in individual bowls. To thicken the soup add 50 g (2 oz) of small pasta shells or rice with the vegetables and allow a few minutes extra. Serve with a sprinkling of grated cheese on top.

Alternatively purée the vegetable soup in a liquidizer or food processor and add 2 tablespoons of baked beans, which will thicken the contents and add some healthy fibre. Reheat in small individual bowls and garnish with chopped parsley for a colour contrast, or swirl a little soured cream on top.

Vegetables, such as broad beans, whole beans, cauliflower florets, leeks, artichokes, can be lightly cooked in the microwave, left to cool, and then tossed in, or served with, a low-calorie dressing. These make simply delicious starters.

Vegetables cooked and combined with eggs and cheese make a satisfying main dish.

Whole vegetables, such as courgettes, peppers, aubergines and whole marrow, can be seeded or cut and sliced as necessary, parcooked by microwave and then filled with

The microwave method of cooking retains moisture and nutrients in food, as well as preserving the colour and texture of fruit and vegetables, thus providing healthy and appealing meals.

appetizing savoury fillings for the final microwave cooking. Mushrooms and large tomatoes can be used in a similar manner but do not require the initial prime cooking.

▨ Cabbage leaves can be parcooked and filled, rolled up and cooked in a spicy tomato sauce.

▨ Ratatouille is easily cooked and is excellent simply served with rice and topped with grated cheese.

▨ Vegetable sauces can be served with many dishes to add delicious flavours. Finely chop the vegetables, add a little stock and herbs of choice and cook until the vegetables are just soft. Purée in a liquidizer or food processor for a smooth sauce and adjust seasoning if necessary.

Fish

Fish is always available, white or smoked fish, fresh, frozen, or even canned. Any fish cooked by microwave remains very moist and so full of flavour that in its simplest form needs only to be served with a wedge of lemon.

▨ In selecting frozen fish, avoid those with a coating of batter or breadcrumbs.

▨ White fish can be marinated in lemon juice diluted with an equal quantity of water, e.g. 2 tablespoons lemon juice to 2 tablespoons water, a few black peppers and dill weed, basting frequently before cooking to impart a delicious subtle flavour.

▨ Fillets or steaks of fish can be cooked with canned tomatoes, finely chopped onions, crushed garlic, chopped parsley, seasoning and served garnished with black olives for a robust flavour.

▨ Fish can be cooked and served on a bed of spinach, topped with grated Edam cheese and a sprinkling of cayenne pepper for a tasty supper dish.

▨ Fish can be cooked and then complemented with a low-calorie sauce. Just mix together a 150 ml (5 fl oz) carton plain unsweetened yogurt, half a teaspoon made mustard, 1 teaspoon lemon juice and a little chopped parsley for a piquant sauce, or if you prefer a sauce with a positive tang, mix together a few prawns with plain unsweetened yogurt, tomato sauce, tomato purée and a dash of tabasco sauce. Both sauces should be heated on Low or Defrost power to prevent a boiling action, and stirred several times during the heating.

▨ The simplest method is to brush the whole fish with a little melted butter or low-fat spread, sprinkle with lemon juice, cook, then serve garnished with sprigs of watercress or parsley.

▨ Whole fish can be cleaned, gutted and rinsed in the normal manner. The cavity can be stuffed with a mixture of low-calorie breadcrumbs, grated lemon rind, chopped parsley and seasoning bound together with a little softened low-fat spread.

Cod steaks topped with Edam cheese and served on a bed of spinach makes a simple but nutritious supper dish.

■ Whole fish can be marinated in lemon juice, sliced onion and bay leaf before cooking, or can be soused in cider vinegar, whole black peppers, sliced onion and celery, a bay leaf and a thick wedge of lemon. This can then be served either hot or cold with a simple salad to accompany it.

■ Canned fish, such as anchovies, tuna, salmon and shrimps, if chopped or flaked and mixed with a little cooked rice and herbs, or sweetcorn and chopped mushrooms, will make tasty fillings for vegetable dishes such as stuffed aubergines, peppers, tomatoes or courgettes.

Poultry

A wide variety of poultry, whole or portioned, fresh or frozen, is suitable for healthy diets, and cooked by microwave the result is moist, tender and full of flavour.

■ Whole birds, when cooked in a roasting bag, do not require added fat, and as the skin does not crisp it is unlikely to be eaten – a bonus for the diet conscious.

■ Cold, cooked turkey and chicken make popular meals served with various salads. Try mixing a little curry paste with slimmers' mayonnaise, and toss in small strips of cold poultry and chopped chives, to serve on crisp lettuce leaves.

■ Cold chicken can be used for such recipes as Chicken à la King and still be low in calories if you substitute low-fat spread, cornflour and skimmed milk for the butter, flour and full cream milk. Yogurt or soured cream can be stirred in just before serving instead of double cream.

■ Poultry portions can be cooked with a variety of vegetables and a small amount of stock to create low-calorie casserole dishes. Alternatively the vegetables can be processed to a purée and served as an accompaniment to the cooked portion.

■ Boneless breast fillets can be marinated in spiced yogurt and orange juice before cooking to impart a delicate spicy flavour.

A moist and delicately flavoured chicken supreme is teamed with asparagus purée for an elegant, low-calorie meal.

They can also be slit at the side to form a pocket which can then be filled with low-calorie stuffings. To cook them, brush with a little fat and sprinkle with paprika or poultry seasoning.

Pasta and Rice

Wholewheat pasta and natural brown rice are included in wholefood diets as a good source of fibre, and if they are complemented with low-calorie sauces or accompaniments they can be eaten in satisfying amounts.

Quantities of up to 225 g (8 oz) can be successfully cooked by microwave, in boiling salted water, with a little oil added for pasta products (see page 57). There is very little saving in time if the recommended standing period is included, but the texture of both are extremely good.

Families who use such foods in large quantities will reap the benefit of a microwave if the pasta is cooked in bulk by conventional means, then stored either in a refrigerator or freezer, and reheated by microwave. This method is far better than any other known method, because the frictional heat created by microwave cooking stimulates the moisture content of the pasta or rice without drying out the food.

The same also applies to pulses, which are highly recommended in many diets.

Fruit Desserts

Fresh fruits are available throughout the year and frozen varieties including soft fruits, plus fruit canned in unsweetened natural juice, afford a wide selection from which to prepare nutritious low-calorie refreshing desserts in the microwave cooker.

Fresh fruits in season, cooked by microwave normally require less sweetening as more flavour is retained. Their natural colour and texture is also preserved.

▪ Fruits can be poached in a small amount of natural unsweetened fruit juice. Fruit whips and mousses can be made by this method.

▪ For fruit fools, cook the fruit and substitute yogurt and a little calorie-free sweetener for the cream.

▪ Whole fruit can be stuffed and baked. Use eating apples as they have a natural sugar content. Core the apples, lightly score around the top. Fill with a mixture of honey, cinnamon and dried fruit, or pack the centre with grapes or blackberries.

▪ To make a crumble topping for 750 g (1½ lb) of fruit, heat 40 g (1½ oz) each of low-fat spread and butter and stir in 225 g (8 oz) of muesli, mixing well to ensure even coating. Layer the fruit in the dish and add some grated lemon or orange rind and 1–2 table-spoons of the juice. Top the fruit with the muesli mixture and heat for approximately 7–8 minutes on Maximum (Full) power. Allow to stand for 5 minutes before serving.

▪ Poach fruits until soft, then process them to a purée and serve as sauces to poultry, meat, rice and pasta dishes.

Uses for Baby Foods

Finally in this chapter on healthy eating, mention must be made of the valuable aid the microwave cooker offers in the preparation of baby foods.

▪ If it is possible use a lower power setting when heating foods as this will control any rapid rise in temperature.

▪ If you do not have a low power setting on your cooker, stand a glass of water in the cavity with the food, as this action will slow down the heating.

▪ Baby foods and drinks should be stirred during and at the end of heating and checked for temperature before serving.

▪ All bottles and teats should be sterilized with sterilization tablet or powder by normal methods.

▪ Nutritious foods such as fish, vegetables, fruit and cereal, can be cooked in small quantities and processed to the required consistency before serving. Alternatively, you could cook them in large quantities then divide them into baby portions to freeze. They can be defrosted when needed in the micro-wave cooker.

▪ To heat glass jars of baby food, remove the lid, heat on Medium power for about 40–60 seconds, stir and test for temperature before serving.

▪ Canned baby foods should be emptied into a suitable dish before heating.

▪ Babies' dried milk can be made up for the daily requirements, kept in the refrigerator and used as required. Heat the milk in a sterilized glass jug on Medium power, stir and test for temperature after 40 seconds, then transfer to the feeding bottle. The actual time needed will vary depending on quantities and type of milk.

Stand a glass of water in the microwave when heating small quantities of baby foods in a cooker which does not have a low power setting.

HANDY HINTS AND MISCELLANEOUS USES

Miscellaneous Aids

The microwave cooker will prove extremely useful in the preparation of many dishes. It can be used in the following ways.

■ To dissolve jelly cubes for use in desserts. Break up the cubes into a small glass bowl, add 50 ml (2 fl oz) water and heat on Maximum (Full) power for 1–1½ minutes. Stir until completely dissolved, then add the required amount of cold water or fruit juice. Leave to set in the normal manner.

■ To dissolve gelatine for use in recipes. Place 3 tablespoons of warm water in a glass bowl, sprinkle in the gelatine and stir. Heat in the microwave cooker for approximately 30 seconds and stir until the gelatine is dissolved. Allow to cool slightly before adding to other ingredients.

■ To make a cup of coffee. Place the water and coffee in the cup. Heat for 1½–2 minutes. Add the milk and sugar and stir.

■ To make lemon tea. Heat the water in the cup for 1½–2 minutes. Add the tea bag and allow to infuse until the desired strength. Remove the tea bag, add a slice of lemon and gently stir before serving.

■ To 'clean' dried fruit. Place the fruit in the bowl and cover with cold water. Heat just to boiling point on Maximum (Full) power. Allow to stand for a few minutes until the liquid cools slightly, then drain and pick off any stalks. The fruit will continue to plump up.

Other uses carried out in seconds

The timings are all approximate because of the many variables of weight, storage and condition of the food.

■ To soften rind on fruit to make peeling easier – 15 to 20 seconds on Maximum (Full).

■ To yield more juice from pressed citrus fruits – 15 to 20 seconds on Maximum (Full).

■ To warm 50 g (2 oz) nuts sprinkled with cinnamon or flavourings – 30 to 40 seconds on Maximum (Full).

■ To warm a slice of cold toast – 15 to 20 seconds on Maximum (Full).

■ To soften 50 g (2 oz) hard packed sugar – 30 seconds on Defrost, breaking up the sugar with a fork. Do not allow to heat up.

■ To dry out 50 g (2 oz) damp salt – 60 seconds on Maximum (Full), with salt on a paper towel.

■ To heat cooled beverages – 30 seconds on Maximum (Full).

■ To loosen frozen mousse and ice cream from individual-size containers – 25 to 30 seconds on Defrost.

■ To soften cream cheese for spreading – 30 to 60 seconds on Defrost.

■ To soften 50 g (2 oz) dry dates for chopping – 30 to 40 seconds on Defrost.

■ To heat jam jars to remove the last of the contents – 30 seconds on Defrost.

■ To melt 100 g (4 oz) toffee for coating – 2 to 2½ minutes on Defrost, with toffee broken into small pieces and placed in a glass bowl.

Drying Herbs

Herbs can be preserved by drying them in the microwave cooker. They keep a good colour and aroma and are particularly useful during the winter months.

Ideally the herbs (mint is shown here) should be clean and dry when picked, but if they need rinsing, gently squeeze as much water as possible from them and pat dry between pieces of paper towel or a clean dry cloth. Pick the leaves from the stems and place on a double thickness of paper towel on the base of the oven. Cover with another double sheet and heat on Maximum (Full) for approximately 3–4 minutes during which time you will see a slight amount of vapour but this will be absorbed by the paper. Turn the paper and contents over halfway through the heating cycle. Allow to cool and make sure they are thoroughly dry before crushing and placing in an airtight storage jar.

Useful Hints on Vegetable Cooking

■ Courgettes and leeks, once trimmed and sliced, need rinsing and draining, but the water adhering to the vegetables is sufficient for cooking. The same principle applies to fresh spinach.

■ Most other vegetables require 2–4 tablespoons of water for cooking.

■ Boiling bags and roasting bags are easy for vegetable cookery as they can be easily shaken or turned over during the cooking cycle. Providing the bag is not opened immediately after cooking they do retain heat for quite a lengthy period. Do remember that bags should be loosely secured with string or

A shallow casserole, covered with a lid or cling film is particularly suitable for cooking vegetables as it can be used for both cooking and serving.

Delicate vegetables such as asparagus or broccoli spears should be arranged in the container with the tender parts towards the centre.

Whole vegetables should be cut or sliced into even shapes for cooking.

a rubber band, to allow a little of the steam to escape. Do not use metal ties on the bag.

▧ Seasoning can be added to the water for cooking but not too much, for the fresh natural flavour requires little addition.

▧ Seasoning and a knob of butter can be added after cooking if preferred.

▧ Stir or rearrange the vegetables during the cooking cycle.

▧ Cook new potatoes in their skins, with a little salted water added to the dish.

▧ Do not overcook vegetables as they continue to cook after they have been removed from the oven due to heat retained.

▧ Vegetables cooked in their skins, e.g. jacket potatoes, should be pricked well to prevent them from bursting, see page 25, and cooked on a paper towel to absorb any excess moisture.

▧ Remember to increase the recommended time if several jacket potatoes are cooked together.

Useful Hints on Cooking Eggs

▧ Tasty snacks and delicious main meals can be cooked with these popular and most versatile of foods, but they do require special care and attention for they cook in such a very short time that a few seconds can make all the difference to the result.

▧ Eggs can also be poached, baked or fried in the microwave oven but they cannot be boiled.

▧ **Never attempt to boil eggs in their shells as the pressure build-up will cause the shell to burst and the egg will explode.**

▧ Eggs have a delicate composition and the yolks have a higher fat content than the white, so they cook at a faster rate. If the yolk is lightly pricked it releases any steam pressure beneath the membrane and prevents the yolk from toughening.

▧ Always watch eggs as they cook because the recommended timings cannot always be accurate. It is advisable to remove them from the cooker slightly undercooked to allow the internal heat to complete the cooking process.

▧ Scrambled eggs, because of the amalgamation of yolk and white are a delight to cook. The finished texture can be controlled to suit every taste; just a few seconds extra cooking will make all the difference between a light fluffy consistency or a firm one.

The timings suggested are only an approximation, as the size, freshness and method of storage does influence these. They are based on using an oven with a 700 watt output power.

To scramble two eggs

▧ Heat a knob of butter in a glass bowl or jug until melted. Beat in the eggs and milk, add salt and pepper to taste, and heat on Maximum (Full) power for between $1-1\frac{1}{2}$

minutes, depending on the consistency required. During cooking, as you see the egg beginning to set around the edges, whisk the mixture very briskly and return to the cooker.

▨ The more times you open the door and whisk the mixture, the easier it is to keep control of the consistency you require.

To poach two eggs

▨ Pour 150 ml ($\frac{1}{4}$ pint) of boiling water, $\frac{1}{2}$ teaspoon of vinegar and a pinch of salt into a shallow glass dish. Bring back to the boil in the microwave, then carefully break the eggs into the liquid and lightly pierce the yolks. Cover the dish with cling film and pierce the top. Heat on Defrost power for 2–2$\frac{1}{2}$ minutes. Allow to stand for 1 minute, then remove from the dish and serve.

To bake two eggs

▨ Coat 2 small cups or individual microwave dishes generously with melted butter or margarine. Break the eggs into the dishes and lightly pierce the yolks. Pour 1 tablespoon of cream or top of the milk over each egg and sprinkle with Parmesan cheese or chopped chives. Cover each dish with cling film and pierce the top. Heat on Defrost power for 2–2$\frac{1}{2}$ minutes and allow to stand for 1 minute before serving.

To fry two eggs

▨ Preheat a browning dish for the time recommended by the manufacturer (usually about 3 minutes). Swirl a little butter or oil on the surface, break the eggs into the hot dish and heat for approximately 1$\frac{1}{2}$ minutes. Use oven gloves to handle the dish.

Handy Hints on Cooking with Cheese

▨ Cheese fondue is easily prepared. Place the selected cheeses and other ingredients into a covered ceramic fondue dish to cook.

A cheese fondue can be cooked in the microwave in a suitable container before being kept warm over a spirit lamp.

Stir frequently during the cooking. A quantity of approximately 450 g (1 lb) takes between 7–8 minutes on Maximum (Full) power. After cooking, the dish can be transferred and kept warm over the spirit lamp. The cheese fondue can also be made in a glass bowl if preferred and transferred to a metal fondue dish after it has cooked.

Cheese, because of its high fat content, melts and cooks very rapidly. If it is combined with eggs in a recipe, it is advisable to use Defrost or Medium/Low power for cooking.

To achieve a golden finish on a recipe coated with cheese sauce, place the finished dish under a hot preheated conventional grill. Welsh Rarebit made in the microwave cooker can also be finished in this manner.

Useful Hints on Cooking Fish

If cooking several at once, arrange the fish fillets with the tails overlapping and towards the centre of the dish.

Allow fish to stand for approximately 3–4 minutes after cooking. It will retain its heat and give you time to make any accompanying sauces.

'Boil in the Bag' fish should have the pouch pierced before heating.

Cook all fish on Maximum (Full) power, unless manufacturers recommend otherwise.

Recipes involving fish in batter are not successful for microwave cooking, as you must not attempt to deep fat fry (see page 39 for further details).

Useful Hints for Cooking Poultry and Game

Whole chicken does colour slightly during cooking without carrying out any of the browning techniques on page 26. Cooked this way it is most suitable for salads, sandwiches or any recipes calling for cooked chicken.

If you want a traditional finish to poultry cooked in the microwave cooker, transfer it to the conventional oven, preheated to a fairly high temperature, for ten minutes or so to crisp the skin and deepen the colour. Do not allow the standing time in this event.

Tie the wings of the chicken as close to the body as possible. A wooden cocktail stick pierced through the wings to the body assists in keeping a symmetrical shape and therefore an attractive presentation.

Wrap small pieces of foil around the wing tips and lower end of the drumsticks to prevent overcooking of these areas. Remove halfway during the cooking cycle.

Invert a saucer in a shallow glass roasting dish, place the bird breast-side down and

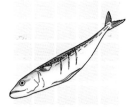

For round fish with skin, e.g. mackerel, lightly score the fish in the thickest part of the flesh to allow the steam to escape. Turn the fish over halfway through the cooking cycle. If cooking two or more, arrange head to tail in a single layer.

When cooking a whole fish, wrap a strip of foil around the tail and head (see page 28) and remove halfway through the cooking. This prevents delicate areas from overheating.

When cooking fillets, fold the thin tail end under the fish to achieve a uniform depth.

cover the dish with greaseproof paper or a split roasting bag. This allows the bird to cook above its own juices. Cook for half the recommended time and turn the bird over for the final cooking period.

■ Alternatively use a microwave roasting rack, as described on page 34. Either leave uncovered, in which case a degree of spattering may occur, or cover loosely. The choice is personal. After testing both methods you will be able to judge which is better.

■ Allow approximately 1 extra minute per 450 g (1 lb) on the cooking time if stuffing is used in the cavity.

■ Standing time is essential after cooking. The bird should be covered in a tent of foil shiny-side down, and left for 15–20 minutes for the heat to equalize.

■ Chicken cooked in sauce can be skinned first if preferred, which will allow the flavour of the sauce to penetrate right through the flesh.

■ If cooking several poultry portions, arrange the pieces so that the thinner parts are to the centre of the dish, where they will receive less energy.

■ Use the power level recommended by the manufacturer for the cooking of poultry and game.

Useful Hints on Meat Cookery

Joints

■ The most successfully cooked joints are of an even shape and free from bone. They should be lean with an even marbling of fat and covered on the outside by a thin layer of fat. The marbling of fat dissolves during the cooking keeping the meat succulent.

■ If a joint does contain bone and is of an uneven shape, for example a leg of lamb, the thinner end should be shielded with aluminium foil (see page 28) for at least half of the cooking time to prevent it from drying and toughening the texture of the meat.

■ Any bone end in a joint and the immediate surrounding area should likewise be shielded, as the meat immediately next to the bone will cook at a more rapid rate.

■ A degree of browning does occur, particularly with the larger cuts of meat which are cooked over a longer period. If you prefer a rich brown appearance, try one of the techniques listed on page 26.

■ Pork rind should be scored and salt rubbed in to crisp the surface. If any part of the skin remains soft after cooking, just cut it off in strips and briefly heat in the microwave cooker; they will soon crackle.

■ All meats will spatter a little during cooking which, as in conventional roasting, is quite normal, but a loose cover contains such particles around the meat, so they do not spread over the cavity walls.

■ Meat should preferably be raised above its own juices when cooking, for which a

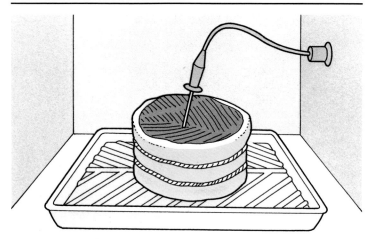

A temperature probe inserted into a joint of meat means that you can judge the cooking by its temperature.

microwave roasting rack can be used. Alternatively the meat can be placed on an inverted saucer or plate in a shallow dish and loosely covered with greaseproof paper or a slit roasting bag. As fat and juices accumulate, remove them and set aside to make the gravy to serve with the meat.

Meat can also be cooked in a roasting bag with the ends loosely secured with string or with a strip from the end of the bag. Pierce the bag to allow some of the steam to escape and place the meat in a shallow dish for cooking.

It is essential that all meats are allowed a standing period of 15–20 minutes depending on the density of the joint. After cooking, remove the meat from the oven and cover with a foil tent. During the first 5–6 minutes the internal temperature will increase several degrees.

If using a microwave thermometer (see page 34) the following is a guide to temperatures. They are based on the internal temperature of the meat on completion of cooking.

Meat	INTERNAL TEMPERATURE ON REMOVAL FROM OVEN	
BEEF (rare)	56°C	133°F
BEEF (medium)	65°C	150°F
BEEF (well done)	70°C	160°F
LAMB	76°C	168°F
VEAL	76°C	168°F
PORK	80°C	175°F
GAMMON	65°C	150°F

Small cuts of meat

These include chops, steaks, sausages, beefburgers or hamburgers.

Because of the fast cooking times, these small cuts will not brown in the microwave cooker unless a microwave browning dish or skillet is used (see page 33). Preheat the dish or skillet for the time recommended by the manufacturer. Once the dish has been heated, coat the surface with fat by swirling round a knob of butter or margarine, before cooking chops and steaks. Alternatively brush melted fat over both sides of the meat before placing on the preheated browning dish. Sausages and burgers contain a sufficient quantity of fat, so this is not necessary.

▨ All foods should be turned during cooking to give a browned finish to both sides and to increase this, flatten or press the food with a spatula, so making firm contact with the dish. Experiment with preheat times as the degree of microwave browning depends on personal preferences.

▨ Remember that a browning dish reaches a very high temperature, and oven gloves should always be used for handling.

▨ Below are a few examples of the cooking times for meats, based on an oven with a 700 watt output power.

Food	Amount	1st side		2nd side
Hamburgers	4	1½ minutes	Turn over	2 minutes
Pork chops	4 medium	3–4 minutes	Turn over	7–8 minutes
Sausages	450 g (1 lb)	2 minutes	Turn over	2½–3 minutes
Steak	250 g (8 oz) 1 cm (½ inch) thick	1 minute	Turn over	1½–2 minutes

Minced meat

▨ This economical variety of meat, with its suspended distribution of fat cooks extremely well in the microwave cooker. It can be used for sauces, such as Bolognese, for meat loaves, meat balls and burgers, although it may be necessary to add a few drops of gravy browning to improve the appearance of some of these recipes.

▨ The coarser ground varieties are most suitable for moussaka and chilli-con-carne and give excellent results.

Useful Hints on Cooking Pasta and Rice

When cooked by the microwave method both pasta and rice give excellent results and clearly show how important the standing time is, as during this period they cook to perfection. There is little, if any, time saving between

Lasagne reheats excellently in the microwave cooker.

this and conventional methods but there are other advantages, such as eliminating the possibility of sticky saucepans, reducing the amount of steam in the kitchen and being sure that the correct texture can be achieved by the simplest of methods.

▨ Cook pasta or rice in a deep dish or bowl to allow for the boiling action of the liquid and the expansion of the food.

▨ The dish needs to be loosely covered with a lid or cling film which has been pierced to allow a small amount of steam to escape.

▨ The principles of cooking are very similar except that you add boiling salted water to the rice and you pour the boiling salted water into the dish before putting in the pasta. It is most important that all pasta is totally immersed in the water before the cooking commences.

▨ For awkwardly shaped pasta, such as spaghetti, immerse the strands gradually into the boiling water and as they become pliable gently immerse the remainder.

▨ For ease of handling cook lasagne sheets in a shallow rectangular dish and remove them with a plastic spatula. If you cook freshly made pasta, reduce the cooking time given in the chart below by approximately one third.

▨ After standing time has completed the cooking, drain the pasta and toss with butter before serving.

▨ The 'easy cook' varieties of rice will, during standing time, absorb all the liquid and can be served immediately.

▨ Long grain or patna rice varies considerably and some types need to be drained and fluffed up with a fork before serving.

▨ Brown rice, which needs a longer cooking cycle, has a period on Defrost/Low power after the Maximum (Full) in order that moisture is retained during the final cooking period.

Hints on Cooking Pulses

With the exception of split lentils, all pulses must be soaked before cooking.

Dry weights of up to 225 g (8 oz) can be successfully cooked in the microwave cooker and will yield about three times that quantity. Larger quantities are best cooked by conventional methods.

The microwave cooker can speed the time of soaking pulses if this is a critical factor. Cover them with cold water, bring them to the boil and cook for just 4 minutes. Allow them to stand for $1\frac{1}{2}$–2 hours during which time they will swell and soften. Rinse thoroughly before cooking.

To cook, place the soaked and rinsed pulses in a dish deep enough to allow for boiling. Pour boiling water over the pulses and cover the dish. Bring to the boil and continue cooking until tender. Timings vary considerably as the age of the pulses determines the

GUIDE TO COOKING PASTA AND RICE

Pasta/Rice	Quantity	Preparation	Cooking time on Maximum (Full)	Standing time
Lasagne sheets	6–8	Use a rectangular shallow dish. Immerse in 600–900 ml (1–1½ pints) boiling salted water with 1 tablespoon oil	10 minutes	10 minutes
Macaroni medium cut	225 g (8 oz)	Immerse in 1.25 litres (2 pints) boiling salted water with 1 tablespoon oil	8 minutes	6–7 minutes
	100 g (4 oz)	Immerse in 900 ml (1½ pints) boiling salted water with 1 tablespoon oil	6 minutes	5–6 minutes
Pasta shells small variety	225 g (8 oz)	Immerse in 1.25 litres (2 pints) boiling salted water with 1 tablespoon oil	7 minutes	5–6 minutes
	100 g (4 oz)	Immerse in 600 ml (1 pint) boiling salted water with 1 tablespoon oil	5 minutes	5–6 minutes
Spaghetti	225 g (8 oz)	Immerse in 1.25 litres (2 pints) boiling salted water with 1 tablespoon oil	9 minutes	6–7 minutes
	100 g (4 oz)	Immerse in 900 ml (1½ pints) boiling salted water with 1 tablespoon oil	7 minutes	6–7 minutes
Tagliatelli and Egg noodles	225 g (8 oz)	Immerse in 1.25 litres (2 pints) boiling salted water with 1 tablespoon oil	6 minutes	5 minutes
	100 g (4 oz)	Immerse in 900 ml (1½ pints) boiling salted water with 1 tablespoon oil	5 minutes	5 minutes
Brown rice	225 g (8 oz)	Add 900 ml (1½ pints) boiling salted water	20 minutes on Maximum (Full) plus 8 minutes on Defrost	7–8 minutes
	100 g (4 oz)	Add 600 ml (1 pint) boiling salted water	15 minutes on Maximum (Full) plus 7 minutes on Defrost	
Easy cook varieties	225 g (8 oz)	Add 600 ml (1 pint) boiling salted water	11 minutes	6–7 minutes
	100 g (4 oz)	Add 300 ml (½ pint) boiling salted water	7 minutes	6–7 minutes
Patna/ Long grain	225 g (8 oz)	Add 900 ml (1½ pints) boiling salted water	10 minutes	7–8 minutes
	100 g (4 oz)	Add 600 ml (1 pint) boiling salted water	8 minutes	7–8 minutes

cooking time necessary. A general guide for the quantities mentioned would be approximately 40–60 minutes, during which period it would be necessary to stir several times. Lentils of the same weight would take approximately 20–25 minutes.

Useful Hints on Fruit

The full flavour and fresh colour of fruit are exceptionally good cooked by microwave and make attractive puddings, desserts and preserves.

▓ Fresh fruit should be prepared in the normal manner and whole fruits such as apples or plums need to be scored or pricked before they are cooked to prevent them from bursting.

▓ Fruit should be poached on Maximum (Full) power in a shallow dish with a cover and stirred or rearranged halfway through the cooking cycle.

To poach 450 g (1 lb) apples or pears

Core and slice evenly. Place in the dish with 2 tablespoons water and 100 g (4 oz) caster sugar. Cook for 4–5 minutes. Allow to stand for 3 minutes.

To poach 450 g (1 lb) plums or greengages

Prick each fruit with a cocktail stick, place in the dish and add 1 tablespoon water and 100 g (4 oz) sugar. Cook for 4–5 minutes. Allow to stand for 4 minutes.

To poach 450 g (1 lb) blackberries or blackcurrants

Place in the dish with 2 tablespoons water and 150 g (5 oz) sugar. Cook for 5–6 minutes. Allow to stand for 3 minutes.

▓ Dried fruit does not need to be soaked before cooking by microwave methods.

To cook 225 g (8 oz) dried fruit

Place the dried fruit in the dish, add a wedge of lemon and 600 ml (1 pint) water. Cook for 7 minutes, stir thoroughly, then add 50 g (2 oz) sugar and heat for a further 7 minutes. Allow to stand for approximately 30 minutes for the fruit to continue cooking and swell. Chill before serving.

▓ Canned fruit can be transferred to a suitable container and successfully heated in the microwave cooker.

▓ Canned pie fillings can form the base of a fruit sponge dessert.

▓ Frozen fruit can be easily defrosted (see pages 50 and 51).

Useful Hints on Puddings

▓ Puddings and desserts are simple to cook by microwave and firm favourites, such as syrup suet pudding, chocolate sponge puddings and upside down fruit puddings, are made in a matter of minutes providing a great time advantage over conventional cooking.

To steam a pudding

▓ Grease the inside of a glass or china

basin and place any required syrup or jam in the bottom.

▪ Carefully spoon the pudding mixture on top and cover the dish with cling film. Pierce two small holes in the top to allow a little steam to escape. Heat for the recommended time, turning the dish slightly if necessary during this period. The mixture will rise very rapidly and it is a pretty sure indication that when it rises to the top of the basin the pudding is almost cooked.

▪ Allow to stand for 5 minutes, then carefully remove the cling film, lifting it from the back of the dish towards you, and turn out into a warmed serving dish.

To cook an upside down fruit pudding

▪ Grease the inside of a glass or china dish.

▪ Melt 25 g (1 oz) of butter or margarine in the base and sprinkle 25 g (1 oz) of demerara sugar evenly on top. Arrange fruits in a decorative pattern. Gently spoon the mixture on top, do not cover.

▪ Heat for the recommended time and allow to stand for 5 minutes before inverting on to a warmed serving dish. During the standing period you will notice that the sponge mixture will shrink away from the edge of the container and slightly reduce in size but this is normal. Serve straightaway.

Fruit retains both colour and texture when poached in the microwave cooker.

An upside down fruit pudding is made in moments.

To make a caramel

■ Allow two thirds of liquid to sugar, i.e. 120 ml (4 fl oz) water to 175 g (6 oz) of caster sugar.

■ Use a 1 litre (1¾ pint) ovenproof glass jug and place in both ingredients. Heat without stirring for 10–12 minutes until a bubbling golden caramel forms. Remove the jug from the cooker carefully as it will be hot, using oven gloves to protect your hands from the spattering which may occur.

■ Quickly stir in 2 tablespoons of warm water and heat for a further 30 seconds in the microwave cooker.

To make a biscuit base

■ Use 75 g (3 oz) of butter to 175 g (6 oz) crushed digestive biscuit and 25 g (1 oz) of caster sugar. Melt the butter in a large bowl on Maximum (Full) power for 1½ minutes, then stir in the biscuit crumbs and sugar. Mix until thoroughly combined.

■ Press the mixture in the base of a 22.5 cm (9 inch) flan dish and compact the mixture with the back of a large spoon until it is quite firm. Place in the refrigerator to set for at least an hour before filling.

To cook a rice pudding

■ Mix 50 g (2 oz) pudding rice, 50 g (2 oz) sugar and 600 ml (1 pint) milk together in a 2.25 litre (4 pint) glass bowl and heat on Maximum (Full) power for approximately 7–8 minutes until the mixture is just boiling.

■ Stir thoroughly, then reduce the setting to Medium power and cook for approximately 22–25 minutes. It will be necessary to stir during this period to prevent any lumps from forming.

■ Remove from the cooker and sprinkle grated nutmeg on the top, if liked. Allow to stand 7–8 minutes before serving, and you will notice that during this time the mixture will thicken considerably.

Useful Hints on Cake Making

▨ Cakes do not brown naturally but many suitable recipes can be made to overcome this disadvantage by using such natural ingredients as chocolate, ginger, coffee, spices and dark treacle to create a rich coloured appearance. Plain cakes can be very often made with soft brown sugar which will give them a golden colour, or they can be finished with one of the colourful decorations listed on page 27.

▨ The texture of sponge cakes is very light. Most conventional recipes can be adapted by adding 2–4 tablespoons of warm water to the ingredients, so that the mixture has a soft dropping consistency before it is cooked.

▨ Most cakes are cooked on Maximum (Full) power unless otherwise recommended by the manufacturer, the only exception being rich fruit cakes which require a slower cooking on Defrost or Medium/Low power.

▨ For rich fruit cakes lightly grease the dish, and coat the sides with a little sugar, knocking out any surplus. Line the base of the dish with greaseproof paper.

  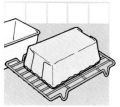

Cakes can be cooked in a straight-sided container, such as an undecorated china or glass soufflé dish, in a special microwave savarin ring or in special microwave moulds or cake dishes.

Check whether the container is suitable before purchasing. Either completely line with cling film, smoothing out as many creases as possible – the cake can be lifted out on to

a wire tray when cooked – or line the base of the container with greaseproof or non-stick parchment paper and lightly grease the sides. Invert on to a wire tray when cooked.

▨ Never grease and flour a container, you will only finish up with an unpleasant looking and tasting floury film around the cake.

▨ Cake mixtures should only half fill the container, so allowing for rapid rise and expansion of the mixture during cooking.

▨ As you turn the mixture into the container, tap the sides gently to disperse any air pockets and always even out the surface.

▨ The inside diameter of the container should not exceed 20 cm (8 inches) but this is quite a reasonable size for family cakes. A wider container which spreads the mixture over a greater area may mean that the centre of the cake remains undercooked.

▨ Cakes rise very rapidly by this method and for this reason many manufacturers advocate rotating the dish during the cooking period. If this is recommended, then in principle it should be adopted.

■ At the end of the cooking period the cake will appear to be very moist, particularly in the centre and very often the temptation is to give it a further cooking. However, this will make the texture too dry. If this should happen, the cake can be broken into pieces and used for trifles or similar dishes. The wet surface will dry out during its natural standing period, by its own residual heat.

■ A fine skewer or a wooden cocktail stick inserted into the cake will test to see if the cake is cooked.

■ Allow the cake to cool in its container for 10 minutes before turning out on to a wire rack and during this period tap the sides gently to help ease the cake from the sides of the container.

■ Convenience cake mixes are quite successful in the microwave cooker and if you follow the manufacturers' recommended methods, providing the mixture has a soft dropping consistency there should not be any problems. As mentioned earlier, if the mixture is fairly heavy adding 2 tablespoons of warm water will make all the difference to the texture.

■ As most of these cakes contain some form of raising agent they cook extremely rapidly, so do allow for this in your timings. An average-sized cake mix around 300 g (11 oz) will take between 4–4½ minutes on Maximum (Full) power.

■ Individual cakes can be cooked in double paper baking cases and arranged six at a time in a ring pattern for cooking, or use a specially designed thermoplastic cupcaker.

Useful Hints on Pastry Making

Pastry can be cooked by microwave, but does differ both in texture and appearance from conventionally baked pastry which generally has wider appeal. The colour can be improved by substituting wholemeal flour for half the quantity of plain white flour. However, when time is short the microwave cooking of pastry has the great advantage of being quick.

■ The rules for pastry preparation are the same as if it were to be cooked conventionally, that is, keep everything cool, don't overmix or overhandle the ingredients and refrigerate the pastry to give it time to relax before baking.

■ Do not cover pastry unless the recipe states otherwise, so that it will have a drier result.

■ Double crust pies or tarts are unsuccessful as the contents cook and bubble out before the pastry is cooked.

■ Vol-au-vent cases are not reliable in the microwave. They cannot be guaranteed to puff up.

■ The best use of pastry in microwave recipes is once it has been baked blind, as in flans and pastry cases. However, details are given below for cooking various pastry types in the microwave.

To cook a flan case Use rich shortcrust pastry for flans and roll out on a lightly floured, cool surface to a circle approximately 5 cm (2 inches) larger than the dish. Wrap the pastry loosely around the rolling pin and ease into the flan dish, gently pressing into shape, but leave 6 mm ($\frac{1}{4}$ inch) pastry above the rim and flute the edge. This helps to allow for shrinkage of the pastry which occurs with rapid cooking.

Chill the flan for 20 minutes, then prick the base and place a paper towel in the case. Cover with dried beans and cook for approximately 4 minutes on Maximum (Full) power, turning the dish if necessary.

Remove the paper and beans and cook the pastry for a further 1–1$\frac{1}{2}$ minutes. Allow to cool before adding any filling.

Rolling out the pastry just larger than the dish.

Wrapping the pastry over the rolling pin.

Easing the pastry into the flan dish.

To cook suet crust pastry Make up the suet crust pastry to a conventional recipe using sufficient cold water to form a soft manageable dough. Knead lightly and form into small dumplings.

For a 100 g (4 oz) weight, place on a well-greased plate, cover with cling film and pierce the top. Cook for approximately 2 minutes on Maximum (Full) power and serve immediately with a meat casserole.

Alternatively they can be added to the meat casserole approximately 5–6 minutes before the completion of cooking.

Suet crust pastry can be used as topping to steak and kidney puddings but the meat has to be cooked first. The approximate timings for such recipes would be 12–13 minutes on Defrost or Low power as this would prevent the liquid content from bubbling through the top of the pastry.

Useful Hints on Baking Bread

As this is the most controversial area related to microwave cooking, two approaches are considered: on the one hand how the microwave can be used successfully to cook yeast breads and on the other how it can assist in the preparation for conventional home baking.

■ Suitable types of yeast bread to cook by microwave include those which are acceptable with a soft exterior, such as baps, soft

The microwave cooker can be used either to cook a loaf of bread completely or to assist in the preparation of one cooked conventionally.

rolls, and soft bread loaves, since bread cooked by this method does not develop a firm brown crust. If you prefer, such breads can be browned under a conventional grill after they are removed from the microwave cooker, but it is rather pointless to preheat a conventional oven to firm and brown the bread as this defeats the object of using a microwave in the first place.

▨ Certain decorative aids can be employed as described on page 27.

▨ Conventional metal bakeware cannot be used, but alternatives would be glass pâtis-serie dishes, flans and soufflé dishes.

▨ Individual rolls should be cooked eight at a time, placed on greaseproof paper on a greased microwave baking tray, and re-arranged halfway through the cooking cycle. The following details explain the basic pro-cedure for cooking a 450 g (1 lb) loaf by the microwave method and an asterisk ** indi-cates where the microwave can assist with conventional home baking. Quantities should be taken from your preferred recipe. The microwave setting is Maximum (Full).

1. Lightly grease a 20 cm (8 inch) glass flan dish and line the base with greaseproof paper.

2.** Add the sugar to half the water and heat in a small jug for 30 seconds. Stir in the dried yeast and leave to activate for approxi-mately 12 minutes.

3.** Place the flour and salt in a large mixing bowl and heat for 30 seconds or until warm, then rub in the butter or margarine finely.

4. Next add the yeast liquid and remaining water to the flour and mix thoroughly to a pliable dough. Always add 1–2 tablespoons of additional water if the dough appears too dry.

5. Knead the dough on a lightly floured surface until it is smooth and of elastic consistency.

6.** Place the dough in the bowl, cover with cling film and prove by heating for 10–15 seconds, then leaving to stand for 10 minutes. Repeat this process two or three times until the dough has doubled in size. It is ready if it springs back when lightly touched with the finger tips.

7. Turn the dough on to a lightly floured surface and knead well until smooth.

8. Shape the dough and place in the prepared container, sprinkle the top with 1 tablespoon of bran or porridge oats and cook for 6–7 minutes, turning the dish once halfway through if it is rising unevenly.

9. Allow to stand in the dish 10 minutes before turning out on to a wire tray to cool.

QUESTIONS AND ANSWERS

As you become more confident and use the cooker more frequently, questions are bound to arise which you would wish to resolve. Perhaps they are listed below.

Q *Why does the base of my cooker get quite warm sometimes?*
A Heat transfers from the food to any part of the container with which it is in contact. This applied heat from the container heats the base of the oven.

Q *Why do some beverages burst over the rim once they are stirred?*
A When heating liquids, particularly those with a milk content, in a relatively confined area, such as a cup, the temperature below the surface is much higher than it is on the surface, so when you put in a spoon to stir, the natural gases escape and spill over the edge of the cup. To overcome this, stir the liquid halfway through the heating, or try stirring with a plastic spoon.

Q *When a recipe states 'cover with a lid or cling film', which should I use?*
A If a dish has a lid use that. Film is recommended when a lid is not an integral part of the dish, or for such containers that are of an unusual design, and a cover is required to aid cooking.

Q *What would happen if I forgot and put metal in the cooker by mistake?*
A You would soon be aware of the mistake, as the metal would cause arcing, i.e. sparking, across the cooker. This disrupts the wave pattern deflected from the metal cavity and creates a random distribution which can seriously damage the electronic components. Remove the container straightaway.

Q *Why is foil recommended and not metal?*
A Foil is lightweight in comparison, but even so should only be used in small quantities (see note on page 28). Therefore it is only recommended for use when the quantity of food is of sufficient weight to absorb all the microwave energy.

Q *Why do some foods 'pop' in the microwave cooker more than others?*
A Usually because they are cooking too quickly or have a gristle content. Where possible reduce the power level and lengthen the time accordingly.

Q *Why don't microwaves come through the glass door, after all you can see through it?*
A The carefully designed fine mesh allows you to see in the cooker but because of the wavelength of microwaves, they cannot escape,

they just bounce off the mesh and around the cavity until they are absorbed by the food or the oven is switched off.

Q *Which is the best way of cleaning my microwave cooker?*

A It is very simple. The walls, base and ceiling of the cavity stay comparatively cool, so food does not stick on to these surfaces but it is important to keep the oven clean. A warm soapy cloth wiped around the whole of the cavity should be sufficient. Always wipe up spillage as soon as it occurs.

Particular attention should be paid to the door seals but do not use an abrasive cleaning agent on these areas.

For any stubborn areas of spoil, heat a quantity of water in a glass bowl to boiling temperature for a couple of minutes, the resulting vapour should then help to loosen the spoil.

Occasionally strong-flavoured foods may leave an odour in the cooker and to remove this, heat 3 parts water to 1 of lemon juice for 5–8 minutes, then wipe and dry the surface with a clean cloth.

Clean the cooking cavity using warm soapy water.

Pay special attention to the door seals.

Q *How often should I have my microwave cooker checked?*

A If a cooker is used correctly and not abused there is no need for a routine check, and no reason why it should not give years of trouble-free service.

Most manufacturers have a very efficient back-up system, and if for any reason a service on your microwave is required it should only be carried out by a qualified engineer or agent from that company.

Stubborn spills can be loosened by the steam from a bowl of boiling water.

Q *How can I test the heat pattern in my microwave cooker?*

A You cannot, as this can only be assessed by geometrical progression under laboratory conditions. Foods are not always uniform in their consistency and this affects how well or otherwise an item heats.

Q *Can I test the output power of my cooker?*

A You can roughly estimate the output power. You need a Celsius thermometer, a litre glass jug and a watch with a second hand to check the accuracy of your timer.

■ Fill the jug with cold tap-water to the 1000 ml level.

■ Stir the water and register the starting temperature.

■ Heat on Maximum (Full) power for 1 minute.

■ Briskly stir the water and register the heated temperature.

■ Subtract the first temperature from the second and multiply the difference by 70.

■ This figure gives you the approximate output in watts of your cooker. As with all electrical appliances the design varies and each manufacturer has his own method of testing the performance of the cooker.

This operation can only give an approximation of output power, it is not intended as a conclusive test.

Q *Can anything be done to overcooked food?*
A Overdone cakes can be used for trifles and overdone vegetables or fruit can be puréed for sauces and that's about all. It is so very important to use the minimum recommended time, for it is easy to extend if necessary, but you cannot change the texture and flavour of overcooked food.

Q *Can you cook more than one food at a time?*
A If you study a microwave recipe you will realize that foods are added at certain stages to ensure that they all receive sufficient cooking time. Separate foods should be cooked individually to ensure even cooking.

Q *Can I reheat more than one food at a time?*
A Yes, providing that they are of fairly even weight and the time is lengthened accordingly.

Q *Why can't antique glass be used in the microwave?*
A Because the tiniest flaw, not always visible to the naked eye, could distort with this form of energy and would shatter. Also it can be of sentimental value, expensive, and very rarely replaceable.

Special stacking rings can be purchased when reheating more than one plated meal. The top plate should be loosely covered with cling film.

Q *Can I stack plates in my microwave?*
A Yes, stacking rings are available from retail shops specializing in microwave accessories, and one plate can be stacked on top of the other for reheating purposes only. The top plate should be covered. There is little gain in this method of reheating as the time has to be extended.

Q *Do microwaves cook from the inside out?*
A This is a general misconception. Cooking takes place within the food, but not from the centre outwards.

Q *Can I dry flowers in my microwave?*
A There is very little known of this process, but certain work has been carried out in the United States of America, where individual flower heads have been lightly covered with silica gel crystals and heated to retain their natural colour. A great deal of experimentation would be required for perfect results to be achieved.

Q *What happens if my microwave is turned on and there's nothing in it?*
A The microwave energy cannot be utilized without food or liquid in the cooker. Overheating of the components could occur and cause damage, although most of today's models have a cut-out device to avoid serious damage.

It is recommended that a glass of water be left in the cooker which will absorb the microwaves should the cooker be accidentally switched on.

Q *Can I warm plates in my microwave?*
A Yes. Just put a little water between the plates and on the top one and heat for ½–1 minute depending on the number.

Q *Can I cook a whole meal in my microwave?*
A Yes, but because you should only cook one food at a time in the microwave cooker it is necessary to plan your meal and cook food in the right sequence as you do in conventional cooking.
Consider the preparation time, the cooking time and standing time, during which food retains its heat. Foods should be cooked according to their density, because the denser the food, the longer it takes to cook and the longer it retains its heat after cooking. Cook the dense foods first, and prepare the others during this period.
Always wrap or cover the food in foil, shiny side down, after it has been cooked, to keep in the heat. Jacket potatoes, if wrapped this way after cooking, will retain their heat for up to 25 minutes. Other vegetables mostly cook in a few minutes and can be prepared just before serving.
Cold sweets and starters can be prepared beforehand, or a simple pudding can cook while you are eating the main course. If food does cool slightly before serving, just reheat for a brief period.

Q *What output power has been used for the timings given in this book?*
A All timings and information are based on a microwave cooker with a 700 watt output power.

Q *Will a microwave cooker replace my conventional oven?*
A No, for there are certain items which give the best results when cooked conventionally, and the quantity of food must also be considered. Use the microwave for the foods which give the best results cooked this way, backed up by the conventional cooker for others. As you experiment you will realize they provide a perfect service for all your cooking requirements.

Q *Are microwaves really safe for me and my family to use?*
A Refer to pages 9 to 11 which cover the safety aspect and read how stringent tests are carried out on microwave cookers. To put the hazards into perspective, as one eminent professor in the U.S.A., who specializes in microwave energy, quoted: 'The odds of harmful exposure from domestic microwave cookers are about the same as getting a skin tan from moonlight'.

NEW DEVELOPMENTS

It now seems beyond doubt that the initial resistance to the new technology of microwave cooking is rapidly disappearing for the sales in Britain outpace every country in the world in terms of annual growth.

Manufacturers are responding to the demand and where a few years ago the selection of models was very limited, today the number exceeds seventy, with new models and product innovations being launched every month. Models incorporating new features are described below.

Dual Level Cooking

Several manufacturers have introduced such models. They allow both the base of the oven and a shelf above it to be used at the same time, so increasing the quantity of food that can be cooked. Although models vary, usually the microwave energy is fed into the cavity through the sides allowing approximately 60% of energy above the shelf and 40% below. Foods which take longer to cook can be placed on the shelf while those that need slower cooking on the base, not unlike a conventional cooker.

This gives you the flexibility of cooking a whole meal in the microwave cooker, but does require careful planning. Follow the manufacturer's guidelines for advice on timings.

A dual level microwave cooker.

A microprocessor
cooker.

Microprocessor Cookers

This type offers several modern features, for
at a touch of a finger you can select consecu-
tive cooking times with varying power levels.
Such models have memory cooking, which
means that 2, 3 or 4 phases can be programmed into the microprocessor at the start
and each phase will automatically operate
one after the other. Usually the last phase of
any programme is set for any recommended
standing time.

Most models have the advantage of a
'delayed start' programme which enables
you to set the time you want the food to start
cooking, to be ready at a time to suit you. You
can also programme a phase to keep the
food warm should you be later than intended.
They include a temperature probe, for the
cooking of meats, casseroles and beverages,
and when the set temperature is reached, an
audible warning is given, and in some cases
the cooker will automatically keep the food at
the warm 'hold' setting.

Combination Cookers

These have the advantage of cooking both by
microwave and forced air, either separately
or in sequence.

91

A combination cooker.

There are design differences between models and some can be efficiently operated using both microwave and forced air together. They are particularly useful for roasting meats and baking cakes.

Some models include a grill which can be used simultaneously with microwave and is an ideal way of cooking chops, steaks, pasta or 'au gratin' dishes. The advantages of combination ovens are numerous since the fast cooking by microwave coupled with the conventional browning covers most requirements of today.

Double Oven Microwave Cookers

There are two distinct types. One is a double unit consisting of a microwave cooker and a separate conventional oven, with the grill usually situated at the top.

The other type is a free-standing cooker, either electric or gas, with the conventional oven topped by the hob and a small microwave cooker usually at eye level.

Either type of double unit offers the great advantage of having the different methods of cooking efficiently close together.

GLOSSARY

ABSORPTION See page 12.

ARCING This is a band of sparks or incandescent light formed when an electric discharge is conducted from one electrode or conducting surface to another.

BALLOONING The pressure build-up of steam as the food being cooked becomes hot and distorts the plastic film. (Refer to piercing.)

BLANCHING To pour boiling water over food to remove skins, or to cook in boiling water for a brief time before freezing.

COVERING Some foods are covered to retain moisture. This also speeds the cooking process. If integral lids are not available, food can be covered with plastic film, or loosely covered with paper towels or greaseproof paper.

COOKING CYCLE This term applies to the total time from when cooking commences, to its completion, when the cooker switches off.

DEFROSTING During thawing, ice crystals in food revert to moisture. By the microwave method the defrost power level releases microwave energy to the food at regulated intervals only. This helps the food to thaw evenly.

DENSITY The density of food chiefly determines the time it takes to cook or defrost; the denser it is the longer it takes. The relative 'density' of a container affects the transmission of microwave energy to the food. Very dense containers have a slowing down effect on this operation and therefore the food takes a little longer to cook. Lower density containers slow down less.

DOOR INTERLOCKS Models vary in design, but all microwave cookers have at least two, but mostly three switches, which lock into position once the door is closed. They are usually located on the door frame and in some models are incorporated in the door hinges. All doors are well designed, electrically sealed, precision units, to ensure that microwave energy automatically goes off the instant the door moves even a fraction of a centimetre.

DOOR SEAL This is built into the door frame in the form of a metal channel which is filled with absorbent material, to further reduce the risk of any microwave energy escaping.

ELECTROMAGNETIC FIELD This is the usual term used to refer to the microwave energy confined within the oven cavity.

ELECTROMAGNETIC WAVES Any form of radiant energy is composed of electromagnetic waves, such as used in radio, television, X-rays, light and heat.

EQUALIZING HEAT A term used to indicate that heat which has been created in the food has the opportunity to spread evenly to all areas of the food. This applies particularly to defrosting.

FLEXING This describes taking the edges of a plastic pouch and shaking the food contents, halfway through cooking or heating in order to equalize the heat.

FRICTIONAL HEAT This heat is created by the rapid agitation of food molecules. Microwave energy produces such heat very rapidly.

HEATING The time cycle used to bring prepared food to an acceptable temperature for eating is described as heating. Cooking, on the other hand, is the process of dealing with raw food.

MAGNETRON See page 6.

MEGAHERTZ A hertz is the unit of frequency, equal to one cycle per second. A megahertz is one million hertz.

MICROWAVE An electro-magnetic wave measuring approximately 12 cm, which is generated from the magnetron at a frequency of 2450 megahertz.

OUTPUT POWER This is the measure of power available within the cooker cavity, by which the food is cooked.

PIERCING When using plastic film to cover food for cooking, pierce the film in two places with a small, sharp-pointed knife. This is sufficient to allow a degree of steam to escape, thus preventing ballooning (described above) of the film.

POROUS When applied to foods this term includes all types which have a structure of small pores or holes, through which microwaves pass rapidly e.g. cakes, sponge puddings, bread. Applied to containers it would include unglazed earthenware; these should not be used as they can become quite hot if placed for any lengthy periods in the microwave cooker.

PRESSURE This is caused by a build up of steam underneath the surface when cooking foods with a tight-fitting skin or membrane. It is necessary to prick or score such foods before cooking, to prevent them from bursting.

PRICKING Foods, such as jacket potatoes, need to be pricked with the tines of a fork in two or three places before cooking. For foods enclosed in a membrane, such as egg yolks or chicken livers, use a cocktail stick for the same purpose. Fruit, such as plums and greengages, can be treated in the same manner. All methods will prevent the food from bursting as it gets hot.

PULSING Microwave energy is pulsed into the cavity, either in a continuous uninterrupted flow on Maximum (Full) power, or on and off in a regulated pattern on levels of variable power use. The lower the power setting, the briefer the period of microwave energy that is released into the cavity; the higher the power setting, the longer the period of energy applied.

REARRANGING It is sometimes advisable to alter the position of foods during defrosting, cooking and reheating. When foods are in the same container, shift those on the outside towards the centre and vice-versa. If foods are in separate containers vary the position of each of the containers. Read manufacturers' instructions to find out whether or not this procedure is necessary in your microwave cooker.

REFLECTION See page 12.

SCORING The outer skin of certain foods, such as cooking apples for baking, needs to be scored first, to allow the release of steam heat which builds up rapidly within the food. Use a sharp-pointed knife and lightly score the fruit all round just below the top.

SHIELDING This is a term used for preventing sensitive parts of food from cooking too quickly. Such areas are covered with small strips of aluminium foil, provided that your manufacturer's handbook confirms that this is permissible in your particular model.

SPARKING See arcing.

SPATTERING Some foods, e.g. those with a high fat content or pulses which are overheated, 'spit' when cooked in the microwave. Covering the food will protect such spoilage from soiling the oven walls.

STANDING This is a very important period of time, necessary for many foods after they have been removed from the microwave cooker. During this time at the end of a cooking cycle the residual heat in the food spreads evenly.

STIRRING This is recommended during cooking and heating to distribute the heat and liquid content evenly.

TEMPERATURE Timings for foods are affected by their starting temperature. The lower the temperature, the longer it takes to cook or heat; for example food taken from the refrigerator takes longer to reach an acceptable temperature, than food at ambient (room) temperature.

TENTING This term is used for the covering of cooked meats and poultry with foil during the recommended standing period, so that their heat is retained.

THERMOPLASTIC This is a general term covering a wide range of materials. Some of these can be shaped into containers, which are rigid in form and virtually transparent to microwaves. They can be used direct from the freezer to the microwave.

TRANSFORMER See page 6.

TRANSMISSION See page 12.

VENTING When a container is covered with clingfilm, it is sometimes recommended that the clingfilm is pulled back at one corner in order to allow a gap for steam to escape.

WAVE GUIDE See page 7.

INDEX

ACKNOWLEDGEMENTS

The publishers would like to thank the following companies for providing equipment for photography:

Anchor Hocking Corporation, 271 High Street, Berkhamsted, Herts; Corning Ltd, Wear Glassworks, Sunderland: Dickins & Jones, 224 Regent Street, London W1; Electrolux Microwave, 345 Stockport Road, Manchester; D.H. Evans, 318 Oxford Street, London W1; Jones and Brother, Shepley Street, Audenshaw, Manchester; Philips Electronics, Lightcliffe Factory, Hipperholme, Halifax; Toshiba UK Ltd, Toshiba House, Frimley Road, Frimley, Camberley, Surrey; Tower Ceramics, 91 Parkway, London NW1.

Photographer: Grant Symon. Stylist: Jill Barber. Food: Clare Gordon-Smith.
Illustrations: Line and Line.